CHANGED BY
GOD

The transforming power of a relationship with Christ

Testimonies from the
WOMEN'S COMMUNITY BIBLE STUDY

Published by Looking Glass Books
Decatur, Georgia

For additional copies, call 404-869-0095.

ISBN 1-929619-14-6

This volume is dedicated to the glory of God—Father, Son, and Holy Spirit—Who promises to change the lives of those who trust in Him.

CONTENTS

Always be prepared to give an answer to everyone
who asks you to give the reason
for the hope that you have. 1 Peter 3:15

Introduction

A sanctuary is filled with women sitting silently as one of their peers rises and walks nervously to the microphone. Not being used to public speaking, she is taken aback looking out at so many faces staring, waiting for her to speak. Though she appears to be out of her element, there is a contrasting measure of confidence as well. As she begins to speak, her halting delivery is more an evidence of normal stage fright than of not wanting to be there. Her confidence grows as she senses that the women in the audience are with her—that they want, even need, to hear her words. She may tear up, but the strength never leaves her. This is a woman who, a year or two earlier, could never have imagined herself revealing the truth about her life. She was perhaps fearful, perhaps embarrassed, maybe confused, even hurt and angry—but now she is no longer consumed by those things because she has found her identity in Christ. She is not perfect, but now she knows that perfection is not the issue. She has met a Savior who loves her in her weakness and has invited her to follow Him into His kingdom of love and wholeness, now and for eternity. This is a woman who, perhaps for the first time in her life, is standing up straight as an adult, and with joy in her heart, admitting, "I once was lost, but now I'm found; was blind, but now I see." This is a woman changed by God.

I have witnessed the above scene more times than I can count, and yet each time it hits me as though it were the first. What is it about someone sharing a story of how God has changed her life that leaves us in awe? Why am I so moved by these testimonies? It's because it happens to people I know—people who are family to me. When we read about the miracle of life-change in the Bible we think, "That could never happen to me or to someone I know." But it does happen—all the time! Jacob, Moses, David, Paul, Mary Magdalene, and the twelve disciples—many men and women in Scripture were changed forever after an encounter with God. Seeing God's life-miracles up close and personal is a constant reaffirmation that God is at work in our day just as He was in the days of the prophets and apostles. When I see despair turn to joy, purpose replace confusion, love replace anger, and faith overcome fear, I know I am in the presence of God. And being in His presence is what leaves me amazed when I hear the stories of my sisters in Christ.

The 500 or so women who attend the Women's Community Bible Study in Atlanta (WCBS) are indeed my sisters in Christ. Some have joined me in leading others to Christ; others I've shed tears with as we prayed through painful issues; and some have preferred a hands-off approach as they dug their heels in on the back row, gradually let their guard down, and eventually stepped forward to become leaders. The lives (including my own) that have been transformed through the ministry of WCBS represent stories of God's grace and mercy. When God changes a heart, it is a very powerful thing.

After sharing their testimonies, women often say, "I can't believe I did that!" But I can believe it. I have seen over and over that when women gather in a loving community, learn to worship God, start to call upon Him in faith, learn principles of kingdom living by studying the Bible, and begin to see their life-issues from a

Biblical perspective . . . they can't not talk about the results!

• In *community* they discover a spiritual family with bonds that grow stronger every day. For women who meet Christ for the first time through WCBS, this community of believers becomes their first spiritual family. For many more, it becomes their first experience at loving and being loved at a truly spiritual level. WCBS is more than just a gathering of individuals. Like any family, it is a melding of strengths and weaknesses with the resulting whole becoming far stronger than the sum of its parts. The greatest strength of WCBS is the bible-based life of this community of faithful women.

• In *worship* they discover their place in the grand scheme of things; that there is a Creator God bigger than themselves who created them for His glory and for their eternal joy. They learn to enjoy the presence of God as He dwells in the praises of His people.

• In *prayer*, they discover a part of God's character they have not heard about. They learn that He is personal and tender, a "papa" who invites His daughters to sit and talk. They discover that prayer is a two-way time of fellowship with the living God—they talk to Him, and He speaks to them.

• In *Bible study*, they discover wisdom—the skill of living according to God's plan. They not only learn how to know God, but how to receive His forgiveness, be filled with His Spirit, and walk consistently on a plane that is in, but not of, this world.

All of the above, accomplished in a fellowship of love and encouragement, gives them a new perspective on life. Marriage, child-rearing, vocation, avocation, self—everything is viewed differently through the eyes of faith in Christ. And when the eyes of faith are opened, the voice of testimony rings clear. That's why I love to hear the women of WCBS tell their stories—because I know what has happened in the weeks, months, or years prior to their speaking. I know God has been at work and a life has been changed.

In 1995, the Women's Community Bible Study published our first small volume, *Touched by God*. It was brief but heartfelt—the prayers and reflections of a faithful band of women who wanted to offer verbal praise to God for His touch in their lives. This book, *Changed by God*, picks up where *Touched by God* left off, offering longer testimonies of how God, through a community of faith, has changed women's lives.

A number of talented and faithful women stepped forward to see this project to its completion. A special thanks goes to Lynn Adams, who willingly compiled all the stories and assisted in editing; she was the glue that held this project together. Also this project could not have been completed without the invaluable editorial assistance of Marianne Craft, Kathy Lee, Sheila Shessel, Nancy Vason, and Margaret Young. Each of these women gave generously of their time and talents as well as prayerful support to the purpose of this project.

Finally, those who contributed their testimonies are the true authors of this book. These women, each with her own story to tell, gave of themselves because they know and love the One of whom this book speaks. We offer our stories here as a testimony to God's grace and as a source of encouragement to others. Our prayer is that they may light a spark of hope in your own life that is fanned into a flame of faith in our Lord Jesus Christ.

Nancy McGuirk
Founder and Director,
Women's Community Bible Study of Atlanta

CHANGED BY
GOD

O N E

When God Changes You . . .

You Are Surprised by God

Now to him who is able to do immeasurably more than all we ask or imagine, according to his power that is at work within us, to him be glory. Ephesians 3:20

We grow up believing in surprises—or at least we should. Hopefully all of us, somewhere during childhood, found ourselves the owner of a new puppy or kitten on Christmas morning. Or saw our parents come through with money for a trip we were dying to take. Or experienced the rush of relief when our parents forgave us for the world's most foolish adolescent act. Part of what parents love to do is surprise their children. And children learn to anticipate the goodness and generosity of parents who do more than anyone imagined.

It's true, not everyone grew up learning that surprises were a way of life. Not everyone learned that grace and mercy from parents were the keys to our survival as children. But whether surprises were a way of life for you or not, there is a transition to be made when we grow up. It is not a transition into an adults-don't-get-surprises world. Rather, it is the transition into a new family led by a new Father. We are not far from wrong when we say that God gives children parents in order to prepare children to know God. The things parents love to do for their children come innately from parental hearts created in the image of God. Our challenge as adults is to continue believing in the grace from which all good gifts and surprises flow.

Granted, when we leave our parents' nest, it's time to grow up. But in a manner of speaking, the Christian remains a child all her life. She turns her attention from earthly parents to a heavenly Father who is full of grace upon grace, who delights to give good gifts to His children. The amazing grace of God is such that His surprises go beyond our wildest imagination. Even if what we think we need doesn't appear, it's only because His surprise of grace is beyond what we could ask or think— and will be revealed in time.

Read the stories of women who were surprised by God—and see if you aren't encouraged to trust anew in the God from whom all surprises flow.

He said to His disciples, "Why are you so afraid? Do you still have no faith?" They were terrified and asked each other, "Who is this? Even the wind and waves obey him! Mark 4:40-41

God Is in the Details

What I am about to tell you is quite incredible. If you can't believe it, I understand completely, because it is hard for even me to believe! God heard me clearly and then responded in such a personal way. He knows what a visual person I am and He loves me.

After Christmas, my son became ill. He had suffered with respiratory problems all of his life, and as spring began, he found it more and more difficult to breathe. In April, Atlanta's pollen count was ten times higher than ever recorded. My son was captain of his lacrosse team that year, and the biggest game of the season was scheduled for April. He did play, but after the game, he said, "Mom, I feel like someone has dropped a piano on my chest." There seemed to be no way to lift the incredible feeling of heaviness that so depressed his breathing, and the medicine he had been taking was no longer effective. We tried other drugs and sought opinions from other doctors. Each doctor told us that my son would just need more time to heal, and the doctor would write out another prescription. Eventually, my son was taking fourteen prescriptions each day. He struggled mightily to continue with his classes and varsity sports but eventually was no longer able to participate in either one. For five weeks, he was physically incapable of continuing his normal schedule of school and sports, and since he was a high school junior, the pressure on him was enormous. He had been thinking seriously about what colleges to apply to during the upcoming fall, and his first choice was his dad's alma mater, which was hundreds of miles north of Atlanta. However, after watching him struggle with his health throughout that spring, I could no longer imagine him attending a college away from his doctors—and my worry intensified.

We decided to rent a house at a beach in South Carolina, hoping that the warm salt air might help him more than anything else, and we took off immediately after school ended that year. The day after we arrived, I took a long walk on the beach alone. I was so tired and still very worried; I desperately longed to clear my head and to somehow be reenergized. As I walked, I began to pray for God's help.

I had prayed for my son and my daughters all of their lives, but on this particular day, I felt helpless and afraid in spite of my prayers. How could my son possibly survive being away from home? Was his condition so serious that he might not even be able to leave Atlanta? My questions and anxiety mounted as I walked. He wanted to attend a university in Virginia so badly, like his father and many older friends, yet I simply could not imagine him being so far away. As I walked, I prayed and pleaded with God to help me through my son's illness. I must have walked two miles when I turned around to head back to our house. As I approached the house, I saw a piece of paper dancing in the wind. It flew upward in a circular motion and then fluttered down to the sand. *There shouldn't be trash on this lovely beach,* I thought as I walked over to pick up the paper. Before crumpling it in my hand, for some reason, I decided to see what was what written on it. Printed at the top of the page, on steno paper, was the name of the medical center for the same university in Virginia, followed by, what appeared to be handwritten notes of a medical student regarding emergency procedures. There were notes on CPR, how to treat fevers, cardiac arrest, and more. I couldn't believe what I was reading, because I never knew there was a medical center at this university. I looked up and down the beach, searching for the person who had lost his notes. Yet, as I looked in the direction the wind was blowing, the only person I saw was an elderly man asleep under a blue and white umbrella. In the other direction, I saw people at least a quarter of a mile down the beach. The young medical student I was looking for so I could return the notes was nowhere to be found, yet I felt sure he was somewhere on the beach.

I returned to the house amazed, not to mention a little frightened by my experience. I asked my husband if there was a medical school at this university and he said, "Yes." Then I checked on my son, and while nothing had visibly changed, I knew without a doubt God had heard my prayers. God had comforted me by letting me know that if my son attended this university, there would be a medical center that could treat him and provide the medical care he might need.

The following fall, my son applied early decision to the same university, unaware of my experience on the beach. I had chosen not to tell him because I didn't want to influence his decision. I was confident that God knew exactly where he was going, and I trusted Him to guide my son.

In December, I wrote my first check to the university's admissions office, absolutely overwhelmed that he was the only male student from his graduating class who had been accepted for "early decision." I know that only God knew how desperate I felt on that windy June day. I can't explain how that one piece of paper found me on the beach, nor can I tell you whose hand wrote those notes, but I am certain that God meant it for me. God had both my son and me in His care all along.

Father, You amaze me with Your love and care in the most intricate details of my life. Thank You!

Gwynie Dennard

But it is the spirit in a man, the breath of the Almighty,
that gives him understanding. Job 32:8

God Is with Us

Shortly after moving to Atlanta, I met a group of friends who were actively growing in their faith. One friend recommended a book on prayer. This book, which I eagerly read, suggested that one of the most obvious ways God speaks to us is in our thoughts. Through this inspirational process, He directs us daily, not only for our own good but also for the good of others. However, if our thoughts toward ourselves or others are negative, they obviously do not come from God; while thoughts of concern, kindness, and helpfulness most definitely do. Our responsibility is to be aware of how He is directing us.

God may direct us through a "tug" to call someone, to write a letter, to perform a helpful deed, to visit an old friend, or simply to pray for someone He brings to mind. I felt compelled to visit an old friend I hadn't seen in years. I came quite close to dismissing this urge because so much time had passed since we had last seen each other. That was when I remembered the book I had just read. "God," I said, "if this thought is from you, please let the situation work out so I can know."

I had only been to my friend's home once, years ago, so I set out looking for her house not at all sure where I was going! Her phone number was unlisted, I didn't know her address, and re-membering directions was certainly not one of my strengths—yet I felt compelled to find my friend. I kept wondering if this urging could possibly be God leading me, or if it was just a human thought coming from out of the blue. As I drove, I mysteriously began to recall where she lived and eventually found myself at a house that looked vaguely familiar. I pulled into the driveway, got out of my car, and timidly knocked on the front door, having no idea who might answer. My friend came to the door. She was alone and in a deep state of grief.

I spent over an hour with her, sharing God's abiding hope and faith. When I left her house, I was convinced that God often leads us through our thoughts; it's just up to us to listen and respond!

Father, thank You for Your breath in me that leads me to Your truth. Amen.

Judy McMillan

*It is to a man's honor to avoid strife, but every fool is
quick to quarrel. Proverbs 20:3*

Signs from God

I came by my strong-willed, hardheaded, controlling genes
quite naturally. My father, who also had a very strong will, and I
struggled often in our battle of wills. I constantly wanted him to
change, and I'm sure he wanted me to change too. Sometimes I
got very angry when he couldn't do what I thought he should. As
a matter of fact, we struggled with each other and our strong wills
all the way up until four weeks ago.

Four weeks ago I woke up to a beautiful fall day. The sky was
blue and clear with not a single cloud. The air was dry, and the
temperature was perfect. But I wasn't so perfect. I had received a
call from my brother two days earlier that weighed heavily on my
mind. My dad was sick, and my brother said I needed to make
peace with him, to resolve our differences. He knew that Dad and
I were struggling; this was nothing new. As I got in my car that
morning to go to my Bible study class, I decided to focus on getting some advice about dealing with this situation. You see, I didn't
want to face it, because I knew my dad and I would just get into
another battle of wills. When I got to class, a piece of paper was
sitting in my seat. This is what it said.

When a hawk is attacked by crows or kingbirds, he
does not make a counterattack, but soars higher and higher
in ever-widening circles until his tormentors leave him
alone.

The hawk is a powerful adversary. If he chose to fight,

no doubt he would win. But he chooses to fly above all the clatter and fuss by spiraling upward.

All of us have people who make our lives difficult, either directly or subtly. Perhaps you are under fire today . . .

The hawk teaches a valuable lesson. The better part of valor is avoiding strife . . . flying above your tormentors. Just drop the whole matter and leave the scene. Fighting, even when someone else initiates the fight, might exact a greater price than you want to pay in defense and counterattacks. If you choose to soar above it all, then you have focused on a loftier goal and have left your opponents to their own devices.

Why not resolve to spiral upward—above and beyond the conflict—into the very presence of God? Time spent with Him makes tense situations more bearable.

From Lessons From the Heart *by Jan Silvera*

Wow, was this a sign?

When my class was over, I felt better. I had discussed my dad's situation, and I had gotten some good advice on what to say to him and how to say it. I got in my car, opened the sunroof, and as I started to drive away, my cell phone rang. It was my brother, calling to tell me that our dad had just died. I was shocked. We hadn't expected him to die, and I was very upset. I drove home and just sat in my car in my driveway, crying and thinking. As I leaned my head back against the headrest and looked out through the sunroof into the bright blue sky, I saw, directly overhead, a hawk, circling and circling until finally he flew off. I looked over on the front seat, and there was the piece of paper with the lesson from the hawk. I couldn't believe it. How did that hawk appear at that exact moment? Then I read the handwritten note on the paper:

> Friends . . .
> *We cannot change another person!* We can only *change ourselves* and how we react to circumstances. When we invite Christ into our homes . . . Big things will happen and hearts will *be changed!*

Now I notice so many signs each day of God's constant presence in our world and in my life. If we take off our blinders, slow down, and become aware, we will see signs of His presence everywhere.

Saturday, ten days ago, as my brother, sister, and I released our dad's ashes into the bay behind his home on another beautiful, cloudless, blue-sky day, we said our good-byes and I felt his presence. At that moment, a lone fighter jet flew overhead, soared upward, and tipped its wing. My dad was a fighter. Coincidence? I don't think so.

Dear Lord, thank You for being with us everywhere every day. Help us to be sensitive to signs of your presence. Amen.

Leslie Ransom

The prayer of a righteous man is powerful and effective. James 4:16

Prayer Works
on All Continents!

We came to the United States from South Africa six years ago. Apart from dealing with living in a foreign country, hardly ever speaking my own language anymore, the hardest part was being without our support system—our families and friends. The tragedy of the situation is, due to the ongoing political unrest in my country, we cannot return there because the environment is not safe for our children.

Less than a year ago though, after much moving around, God planted me in Madison, Georgia. Shortly thereafter, I was invited to a Bible study group, and I think it is an understatement to say that that's where God began His work. In this incredible group of women He gave me a base of friendship and family. He also placed me here because He had work to do in all these families.

At the end of January 2001, after walking around with lumps in my neck for quite awhile, I had them checked out. Right from the start, the three doctors I saw all prepared me for the worst, which was lymphoma, because I had all of the significant symptoms. The very first day, I didn't even realize the gravity of the diagnosis, because I wasn't sure what word *lymphoma* translated into in my language. Then I saw the faces and reaction of my friends as I told them my diagnosis.

The seriousness also struck me when the doctors became so urgent in their demeanor. The surgeon removed three lumps from my neck. Afterward he told me he has never removed three lumps; one is usually plenty for diagnosis. Extra pathology tests were also sent to a second hospital to confirm my condition. Even my CAT scan was scheduled on a Sunday morning at the crack of dawn. On all my forms they wrote "lymphoma and/or Hodgkin's disease" in the diagnosis box.

Needless to say, you can imagine the emotional roller coaster I was on during that time. Most difficult of all was looking at my three precious children and not knowing what lay ahead. By God's grace, all of this happened while we were studying the chapters of faithfulness in our Bible study. God led all nine of us every step we took during that time, through every question we asked. He also tore down every barrier so those women could be available to me and my family during that time. Suddenly they had time to carry me emotionally, to care for and keep my children during all the numerous appointments and surgery—time none of us has otherwise. God gave me a family, and our friendship grew instantly. More tendrils reached out from the Vine—intense prayers went up for me from the Bible study group in Atlanta, from all of the South Africans living in Atlanta (most whom I'd never met), and of course, from my family across the Atlantic.

During all of this, my big moment of peace came on the surgery table on Valentine's Day. Two nurses and the anesthesiologist did everything they could to prepare me for the surgery. As I was just lying there waiting, with the room beginning to spin, a big male nurse came into the room and said, "I am going to take care of you today. I want you to know that I went through the exact same thing you're going through now, and I received the worst news, that I had lymphoma." Then I felt his hands on my face as he said, "Look at me. I am fine; I am doing just fine." I never saw him again!

Finally, when all the final results came back, everything was *negative.* The surgeon was completely mystified. The hematologist said twice that he'd bet the farm on the fact that I had lymphoma or Hodgkin's disease.

I realize every day that God saved me for a purpose. Nine families—husbands, wives and children—were touched by His awesome power. Every person who prayed for me here and in South Africa realized again the incredible power of prayer.

Sometimes God does not answer our prayers as we expect Him to. I have changed my expectations. If the whole purpose of my life is to learn to love God and to show His compassion to the world, then what He is doing *in* me is more important than what He is doing *for* me. I am also humbled and so very honored to be chosen by God to carry His message of love and hope to everyone I know. Let us always remember that life is to be lived moment by moment and that God is our only guarantee. And if you ever doubt, just look at me and remember, God is still very much at work today; miracles do not just happen in Matthew and Luke. To God be the glory!

Father, thank You for the power of prayer and for revealing Yourself through this miracle. Amen.

Ansie Schoeman

The Counselor, the Holy Spirit, whom the Father will send in my name, will teach you all things and will remind you of everything I have said to you. John 14:26

Completely Loved

When I was a child my family did not attend church, so I asked my parents to drop me off each Sunday. One Sunday the Lord Jesus spoke to me. He told me to walk to the front of the church and give my life to Him, and I did.

Many years passed, and I drifted away from the Lord. I married an unbeliever and had a child, but the marriage was an unhappy one. We divorced after eight years of marriage.

Later I fell in love with another man, and he fell in love with me. We married and later moved to Atlanta. By this time we had three children, and my husband was traveling and working long hours. We went to church every Sunday, but I felt alone and powerless.

One night we quarreled and I began to pray. I no longer had any desire to live, and I asked the Lord to take my life. Several days later, in church, the minister asked for volunteers to deliver surplus groceries to the poor. The Lord spoke to me, saying, "Do this." It was hard work. My heart hurt to see the poverty, hunger, lack of blankets and firewood, and the sickness.

I began to read the Bible. I saw verses about someone called the Holy Spirit. "Who is the Holy Spirit?" I asked the Lord. During a weekly Communion service, a lady from our congregation began to talk about the Holy Spirit. She shared some of her experiences, and when I expressed interest in learning more about the Holy Spirit, she said she would bring me some books. She kept her promise, and I eagerly read the books. I noticed that one book said that the Holy Spirit is a person and that He is the *power* given to help us live a holy Christian life. When I finished the book I asked the Lord Jesus to fill me with the Holy Spirit.

Then I attended a "Faith at Work" conference where many classes were offered. I noticed a session on the Holy Spirit and signed up for that one. The teacher told us the same things I had learned from the book my friend had loaned me. He invited those who wished to receive the "fullness of the Holy Spirit" to stay after class; everyone else could leave. I decided to stay. The teacher instructed us to completely surrender to the Lord while he prayed for us. He asked us to let the Lord have our whole body, including the tongue. As the teacher and another man laid their hands on my head, I felt the strong presence of the Lord, and I began to speak in another language that I had never learned! I felt completely loved for the first time in my life and was filled with joy.

It's been over thirty-one years since I asked for and received the fullness of the Holy Spirit. I wanted the power to live a Christian life, and He gives it to me. The Holy Spirit's power is available to all who ask.

Thank You, God, for giving us Your Spirit to remind us of the words of Your Son, Jesus.

Jimmie Walters

*"My house will be called a house of prayer
for all nations." Mark 11:17*

A Call to Prayer Ministry

A friend invited me to Women's Community Bible Study in the spring of 1992, and I joined the following fall. This was a spiritual marker in my life. It began my growth in the Word and deepened my understanding of God's work in my life. My spiritual growth took on a new dimension when we studied how to experience God. Up to that point I did not fully and clearly understand how God worked in our lives to lead us according to His will. The study laid a foundation for discerning God's will and understanding how God speaks to us.

The next marker was in 1994 when the Billy Graham Crusade came to Atlanta. As head of Operation Andrew at Peachtree Presbyterian Church for the crusade, I was responsible for implementing prayer coverage. For the first time in my life I began to understand just how much some people valued prayer when I saw the hundreds of thousands of intercessors the crusade recruited to cover the event. I committed to growing in my understanding of God's purposes in prayer.

Making good on that commitment, I traveled to Los Angeles in 1995 to attend Bill Bright's Fasting and Prayer Gathering. This was my first time to really fast. I joined with four thousand other believers to pray for revival in our nation. The Lord moved powerfully in my life over the next year in response to my attendance at the gathering. He drew me deeper into the work of prayer and my experience of His presence, love, and faithfulness was amazing.

After the Fasting and Prayer Gathering, He led me to teach a class on prayer. I grew tremendously in my understanding of prayer as I prepared the class lessons. Then, through His Spirit, the Lord empowered me to teach the class. I continue to teach this class, always with fresh insight as the Lord continues to reveal Himself and his ways through my time in prayer and reading the Word.

Over the next few years it became obvious that the Lord was leading me deeper into the work of intercessory prayer. Specifically, I was led to pray that Peachtree Presbyterian would establish a foundation of prayer to undergird all the pastors and ministries. The Holy Spirit kept prompting me with the verse Mark 11:17: "My house will be called a house of prayer for all nations." The Lord brought four dear women to faithfully pray with me for the needs of the church week after week.

Several other members of WCBS met with me regularly before Wednesday teaching to pray for the study and members' personal prayer requests. We saw many wonderful answers to prayer. These women encouraged and supported my call to intercession and covered me and my family with their prayers.

In 1997, the prayer ministry committee was established. The Lord has worked through this committee to lay a foundation of prayer throughout the life of the church. In March 2001, the committee sensed the Lord was leading us to spend a year as a congregation focusing on prayer. On January 6, 2002, the senior pastor of Peachtree designated 2002 as a year of prayer for the church. This was an answer to years of prayer, an incredible journey of experiencing the Lord and His faithfulness. Yet, it is only the beginning of what He wants to do. I am learning to let God be God, and I ask Him to do that which I cannot even imagine to ask. It is the most amazing gift to experience answered prayer as the living God works in and through you to accomplish His will!

Father God, thank You for the privilege to be a part of Your house of prayer!

Sharon Wilson

I consider everything a loss compared to the surpassing greatness
of knowing Christ Jesus my Lord. Philippians 3:8

Having It All,
Yet Having Nothing

My life with Christ began when I was thirty years old. Unlike many who find Him in the valley, I found Him upon the highest mountaintop. At least that is what the world would have called it. I became a Christian when I was at a point in my life where I had attained everything I ever wanted. I had married the man of my dreams. He was gorgeous, funny, and successful. We had a healthy, bouncing baby boy. We lived in a beautiful home and drove luxury cars. I spent my days playing tennis, having lunch with friends, and traveling with my husband. On the outside, life was grand, but on the inside something was wrong.

If anyone had peeked at my heart and known how I was feeling, he would have called me the biggest spoiled brat. He would have wondered how someone could be so unsatisfied when she seemingly had it all. Yet there I was, sitting alone on my bed one summer night, and I was crying. The only thing I remember thinking was, *What is wrong with me? I have everything. Why am I so empty?* It was not as if I was praying or really seeking an answer; I just remember thinking those thoughts.

And then, out of nowhere, something happened. A complete peace and warmth came over my whole body. It was so comforting. I remember just wanting to lie there and not move. And I remember a voice, not audible but inside my mind, saying, *I'm so glad you finally asked. I've been waiting on you.*

Never in a million years would I have said I had just heard the voice of God. I didn't jump up and scream, "I've been saved!" I didn't even tell my husband that I had been crying. I just know that at that moment my life changed forever. I got up from my bed and went to the bathroom to wipe away my tears; for some odd reason, I felt that everything was going to be okay.

In the weeks that followed, I had this unbelievable desire to start learning about God. I bought a Bible and started reading. I later made an actual profession of my faith, where I asked God to forgive my sins and made a commitment to Christ. I joined a Bible study, which gave me a group of friends who could encourage me to grow in my faith. My personal relationship with Christ, which I had often heard Christians speak of, grew incredibly as I began to read and pray and hear the stories of others.

I'll never understand why I heard God's voice that particular night—why that was the time for me. But I know my experience was real, and I would tell anyone who asks that God is undoubtedly real. He has inexplicably given my heart a peace and a satisfaction that the things of this world were never able to do.

Lord, thank You that You allow us to know You through the gift of salvation of Your Son, Jesus Christ. Nothing in our lives compares with the greatness of knowing You.

Margaret Young

T W O

When God Changes You . . .

You Begin to Set Priorities

*But seek first his kingdom and his righteousness,
and all these things will be given
to you as well. Matthew 6:33*

Deciding what you're going to do in the next hour is easy—so is the next day, week, even month. Our lives have enough commitments and responsibilities built into them that we can run on autopilot without stopping to think deeply about what we are doing and where we are going. Our decisions tend to be reactive instead of proactive. Sometimes we don't even like to think beyond the immediate future because it scares us. We know that choices lead to decisions, and decisions reflect our priorities. And if we're not sure what our priorities in life are, then we feel insecure about decisions and choices.

In our American culture it's easy to live an entire lifetime without establishing priorities. If we want it to, our culture will set our priorities for us. We can stay completely busy with careers, shepherding children all the way through college, trying to keep our marriage together . . . and then we wake up one day and wonder if that's all there is. Maybe we've grown lonely, maybe we lose our parents, or maybe we experience a crisis of health or finance. Something makes us look at life and ask, "Is this a life I have chosen or one I have resigned myself to?"

While that is a good question, it is also a dangerous one. Some people who ask that question decide to throw off everything they think has been issued to them—responsibilities, morals, traditions—and strike out to rewrite the script of their future. Others who ask the question come to the realization that establishing the highest priority is the key to ordering the rest. Putting God in His rightful place has a way of making situations we thought were prison doors become open doors to freedom and fulfillment. Allowing God to infuse life with meaning results in everything taking on a brand new perspective.

In this section, you'll read the stories of women who discovered, in myriad ways, that knowing God is life's highest priority.

But the fruit of the Spirit is love, joy, peace, patience, kindness, goodness, faithfulness, gentleness and self-control. Against such things there is no law. Galatians 5:22-23

A Matter of the Heart

Although I have been a Christian my entire life, only over the last ten years have I begun to learn what that means and to really aspire to bear the fruit of the Spirit that Jesus promises us. While doing the right thing was always important to me, it went against my nature. I attended church and Sunday school every week and even became an elder in our church. But I noticed other people who seemed to lead more from their hearts, and I knew that I was missing out. For me, Christianity was just a "head" thing, not a matter of the heart.

I worked full-time as an attorney and had three growing children. Life became more and more hectic, and my doubts about what I was doing increased. My mother was diagnosed with lung cancer, and I began making biweekly flights to Connecticut to be with her. Then my four-year old nephew died unexpectedly, and I knew that something had to change. There wasn't much I could do except pray, which I was learning to do on a regular basis. I realized then that I needed to quit work and redirect my life toward family and Jesus Christ. I visited my mother soon after and told her of my decision. Her joy was intense, as was my own. She died three days later.

I moved ahead with my decision to quit my career and have never looked back. The first thing I did was sign up for Women's Community Bible Study. This was the beginning of the journey to unlock my heart. Change didn't happen overnight, but the wonderful fact is that the better you come to know Jesus Christ, the more you want to know Him, to be filled by his Holy Spirit, to love Him and to be loved by Him. Daily prayer begins as a discipline but becomes a foundation of daily life. Bible study becomes more than just an activity to squeeze in at odd moments; you learn to schedule it as a daily priority.

My message is that God will sustain us no matter what. When the time is right, He will do whatever it takes to make us right with Him. In my case, God softened my heart and helped me look beyond my anger to the underlying hurt. I have learned to give all my life—including my pain—to Him. I know that each day will be a struggle to keep the ground I have gained, but my confidence in the power of our Lord helps see me through. Each day I go to Him for renewal and strength. I know I can call on Him for help no matter what difficulty I face.

Lord, thank You for the fruit of Your Holy Spirit, which includes the self-control to enjoy all of the other blessings.

Gaylen Baxter

Love the LORD your God with all your heart and with all your soul and with all your strength. These commandments that I give you today are to be upon your hearts. Impress them on your children. Talk about them when you sit at home and when you walk along the road, when you lie down and when you get up. Deuteronomy 6:5-7

Transgenerational Blessing

The idea of God as a heavenly Father who loved me beyond measure was easy for me to understand, given the example of my own father. I thought Dad was just like Jesus; he loved me even when there was little about me to love. As I watched how he lived his life, I realized that the choices and decisions he made were born out of a profound trust in the truth of everything the Holy One has done and said.

To model Christ for a child in such a way that when you are gone that child can say, "I know what God would want me to do because I know what Dad or Mom would do," provides a touchstone for the next generation. For me this is the definition of transgenerational blessing. When you need to experience "God with skin on," having memories of parents who demonstrate that example is a gift beyond measure. Each of us as Christians has the highest calling to pass down such an inheritance to every child God has placed in our lives.

As a young adult, one of my persistent questions was, *Isn't there more to a relationship with Christ than the form and ritual of the church?* I began a quest to discover that "something more." The explosions of life will throw you into the arms of the waiting Savior faster than anything, and that was my experience. My prayer of salvation was, "Help me, Lord. I cannot do this by myself."

The Bible is the story of God's pursuit of an intimate relationship with everyone who is willing to receive Him; it reveals our Father's desire for relationship with us. Examining life's challenging questions in light of that fact, with women who daily seek to know Him better, has become pure joy for me. My children will tell you that they have been raised, in part, by every small group I have ever belonged to in Women's Community Bible Study. A women's Bible study is a perfect vehicle for transmitting blessing to the next generation of children. In such a group women come to realize that even if they did not receive the blessing of a Christian heritage from their own families, our God is a God of renewal and restoration. Even today through Christ they can establish this tradition in their own families and let it stand as their legacy and blessing to their children.

If, by God's grace and His power working in me, I am able to give my children a glimpse of our Savior and in turn see that they will do the same for their children, and if I can encourage a woman in my Bible study group to stand for Christ in her family, then I will feel I have accomplished what God placed me in this world to do.

Heavenly Father, thank You for the blessing of growing up with a godly father. Help me to be faithful to impress my children to love You with all their hearts, souls, minds, and strength. Amen.

Janet Burrell

I have come that you might have life, and have it
abundantly. John 10:10

Abundant Life

For years people invited me to prayer breakfasts and Bible studies. Even though I felt like I loved God, I wasn't sure I wanted to publicly display that love. I'm not sure how I judged people who attended such gatherings, but I decided that I didn't want to be one of them. Interestingly enough, I could feel God trying to draw me closer to Himself, but I ran the other way. I wanted warm, fuzzy feelings of God on Sunday morning; I even wanted a "good word" for the week; but I didn't want God in my face or in my business on Monday through Saturday! I thought that I could "do life" by myself. I wanted God's help when I needed Him, during times when I felt helpless. But soon I would feel better and get back in control, or so I thought.

The day came when a specific event in my life literally took me to my knees. But as devastating as it seemed at the time, the experience was a blessing in disguise. It put me in a position that allowed God to penetrate my stubborn heart. The One I considered to be my Father and Savior was soon to become my Lord and great Counselor.

A friend gave me a set of tapes that especially spoke to me at that point in my life. A year later, another friend invited me to a Bible study, and that time I was ready to go. What I began to learn about God, myself, and others has been the greatest adventure of my life. I am learning the meaning of "letting go and letting God have His way." That's not an easy concept to learn, and applying it doesn't happen naturally. It is a process you learn as you begin to trust the unseen Creator of the universe.

Apart from knowledge of God, we can feel like we're up against the impossible storms of life. We feel defeated and hopeless. But life doesn't have to be that way. The more we learn about God, the more we want to know Him. And the way to know Him is to learn what He says about Himself and how He relates to others. We find this information in His Word, the Bible.

Through Women's Community Bible Study, I am learning to apply God's Word to my daily life. That's the most exciting and fulfilling part of all. My life isn't perfect, but it's better, and I'm a better person in a number of ways. Isn't that what most of us want—a better life—however that might translate for each one of us? We can have an abundant life. Isn't that what we need? If we want it, all we have to do is ask.

Gracious Father, help us receive the abundant life You offer through Your Son.

D.D. Cardwell

The peace of God, which transcends all understanding, will guard your hearts. Philippians 4:7

Learning to Let God Be My Palm Pilot

As a member of Women's Community Bible Study, I have discovered the importance of growing in a true relationship with Christ. I have come to realize that the Lord God Almighty is holy, omniscient, merciful, forgiving, and full of grace. Numerous gentle reminders of His presence have become undeniably apparent during my ten years in this Bible study. Women congregate each Wednesday morning to be still for two and a half hours (amazing, huh?), focusing on God's Word as they disembark from their carpool lines, ongoing agendas, or continuous pulls of the world. These mornings at WCBS have become times to place my heart, soul, and mind in God's "Palm Pilot" rather than my own.

Often my tendency to be a purpose-filled woman can lead me off track from God's desires for my life. I am blessed by believing in the Lord, seeking to know Him better, and being transformed by Him. (Thank goodness He isn't done with me yet!) When I open myself to seeking God's will, I undoubtedly feel God's gentle taps or sometimes forceful arrows shooting straight into my heart.

Learning what true relationships are and treasuring their value more than anything else are key benefits I have gained from my growing spiritual journey as I place myself in His hands. I trust God, have faith in Him, and know He is the author of my life. My core relationship with God rests on learning and applying His Word. My relationship with Him becomes the foundation of my relationship with my husband and children, as well as with other dear friends. One of these friends serves as my prayer accountability partner. We continuously talk, share, laugh, cry, and pray for our dear husbands, eight (combined) children, and ourselves. This fellowship has developed purely through releasing our concerns to the Holy Spirit. I am blessed to be surrounded by unconditional love, which clearly exemplifies God's grace, power, and strength.

Each new day, I can relinquish the role of planner and overseer to God because He is willing and able to plan and guide everything. When I get out of His way, I can give each day to Him and thank Him for each day. He pilots my life so much better than I would ever be able to; He is so much more efficient than I could ever be. In order to know what God desires for me, I must listen and focus my attention on Him. Sitting still on Wednesday mornings, studying, and praying are practices that enable me to put God in charge of the agenda He desires for my heart, soul, and mind. For that peace I am so grateful.

Lord Jesus, thank You for the peace that comes when we allow You to pilot our lives.

Indy Cesari

For it is by grace you have been saved, through faith—and this is not from yourselves, it is the gift of God—not by works, so that no one can boast. Ephesians 2:8-9

Understanding Heaven

I would like to share my personal lifetime experience of getting to know Jesus Christ. I say lifetime, because as far back as I can remember I have loved the Lord. To give you a little background, I was raised as a Catholic in a family of seven. I had a wonderful childhood with parents who really loved me. My parents enrolled me in Catholic school for grades 1 through 4. I think that because of my Catholic upbringing, I grew up loving everything about God, praying, and doing things that I knew would please the Lord.

In junior high school I went to a Billy Graham Crusade with "born-again Christians," as they called themselves. I was a little wary of how they approached God, but I did want to check things out. As a result, because of my love for the Lord, I went forward at the altar call. But I still don't think I grasped everything at that time.

Things became a lot clearer to me in college. I became involved with a Bible study at my sorority. I found out I needed to settle a major question in my life, and that question was, *How can I be sure that when I die, I'll go to heaven?* Up until that time, I had always strived to be the best person that I could be. I tried hard to obey the Ten Commandments, and when I did commit a sin, I would go straight to confession and confess it. But I began to wonder, *What would happen if I got to heaven and the Lord said to me,*

"And you think that was a good job? Well, it was far from it, and you are going to hell."

I finally got that question answered; I found the answer in God's Word, the Bible, which He inspired people to write all so that we all might know about His plan of salvation. I discovered that I could never do enough on my own to merit getting to heaven. All of my good works, trying to please my parents, following all the rules—all of this would fall short because I would never be perfect, and God requires perfection. But what I found out was this: Jesus Christ died on the cross to pay for my sins. He did this so that I could have eternal life with God. All I needed to do was believe and receive Him into my heart. All He required in return was that I turn my whole life over to Him—to make the commitment from that day on I would live to serve Him, not just myself and my own desires. I would go where He says go, whether it's comfortable or not. When faced with a decision, I would always go to Him first and ask, "Jesus, what do you want me to do in this situation?" And that's what I've done with my life. I really don't know where I would be today or what I would do if it weren't for my friend Jesus going before me and helping me every step of the way.

In addition to His Word, I believe that God sends certain people into our lives to encourage us and to help direct us down the path that He wants us to follow. This is what Women's Community Bible Study has done for me. The friendships and the sharing with other women have encouraged me and helped me through the birth of my premature son, the death of my older brother, and my walk of faith. The most powerful thing I have witnessed is the tremendous ways God has answered prayer requests that the small groups have prayed about. We see God dramatically at work in our lives, and

He receives all the glory. And when we all worship Him together in song, I feel a taste of heaven right here on earth.

Father, thank You for giving us saving grace through Your Son, Jesus Christ. Give me the faith to accept this awesome gift and the assurance of eternal life with you. Amen.

Janet Gannon

The Spirit of the Sovereign Lord is on me, because the Lord has anointed me to preach good news to the poor. He has sent me to bind up the brokenhearted, to proclaim freedom for the captives and release from darkness for the prisoners . . . They will rebuild the ancient ruins and restore the places long devastated. Isaiah 61:1, 4

Journey of the Heart

In the fall of 2000, after many months of trying to "fix" my family of origin, I became severely depressed. While I knew in my heart that God would meet me in my depression, I wanted desperately to withdraw and do nothing. During this difficult period, a dear friend approached me about a wonderful Bible study she had been attending. Because of her support, encouragement, and prayers, I eventually joined Women's Community Bible Study, which continues to be a vital part of my life. Then, thanks not only to my faithful friend's suggestion but to God's spontaneous intercession and guidance, I began another individual Bible study at home. I was seeing a Christian psychologist at the time and will never forget taking the study book with me to one of our sessions. After looking over the book, he made a profound remark that had a remarkable impact on me: "If you are going to do one more thing with your head, throw this study down now! However," he said, "if you will do it with your heart, I believe it will really be good for you." At that moment God opened my heart and gave me ears to listen. My immediate prayer was to ask God to change my heart, not just my thinking. The psychologist then observed that I needed to find the "little girl" in me and set her free.

Not long afterward, as I was working on the Bible study workbook one day, my neighbor called. She wanted to know if I would accompany her and her children on a weekend trip to North Carolina—very close to the small town where I grew up. God miraculously took care of every excuse I could come up with to avoid the trip, so I *knew* He was calling me to go! The night before I was to leave, my husband even said, "You need to go get the little girl and bring her back home." Oh boy! I really didn't want to go then.

My first morning when I awoke in my childhood home, I felt drawn to immediately begin work on my Bible study, which I had brought with me. The lesson was on our failure to believe in God's unfailing love. Thanks to the notes at the end of the session, I was able to pray according to the Holy Spirit's direction: "Father God, forgive me. Help me with my unbelief. Take this little girl in me out of unbelief, and into Your loving arms, helping her to embrace You, Your blessings—and to choose life. Thank You."

The next morning I was even more anxious to work on the study, and I opened to a lesson on love. This lesson focused on whether or not we believe we are loved. I was really amazed by this exercise. At the end of the day, I was to complete the study by reading 1 John 4:16. I have come to know and to believe the love that God has for me. The words of that Scripture were brand new to me, and I *finally* knew that God, in His unfailing love, had set me free. My heart was changed. He had gently brought me to the very home where I had grown up and was binding up my broken heart, freeing me from the captivity of unbelief. Before that experience, I would have argued vehemently had anyone told me that my *sin* was my *unbelief,* because I had received Christ as my Savior when I was nine years old and had always believed His love for me—in my head. I now understood that what He really wanted was for me to *know* His unfailing love for me *in my heart.*

Jesus has been rebuilding the ruins of my heart since this powerful event. So much has happened since my journey home that I feel *compelled* to share the miraculous way in which He has set me free—not to mention the unshakable hope and faith I have in Him. My faith will not disappoint (Romans 5:5). I know this because His Word says so!

Father, Your Word assures me of Your love and grace. Fill me with Your Holy Spirit, that I might share Your good news with the poor, the brokenhearted, and those who live in darkness so that they may experience Your eternal love and light. Amen.

Kim Johnson

*"So, now go. I am sending you to Pharaoh to bring my people the
Israelites out of Egypt."... And God said,
"I will be with you." Exodus 3:10, 12*

Trust and
Obey

I began my journey of faith years ago—the faith one learns
through crisis. I suddenly became widowed with a baby daughter.
Years later when that daughter became an adolescent, there were
many times when I thought I would lose her too. She suffered
from bulimia, depression, and was generally out of my control.
But I felt God's presence throughout those turbulent times. He
taught me to trust Him through those frightening years.

I thought I had learned to "let go and let God." But as my
daughter recovered and grew up, our relationship was beautifully restored. I settled into another happy marriage and grew
complacent.

I was involved in my church in many areas and was active
with the Buckhead Christian Ministry. But I also had a career of
thirty-three years that kept me away from home a couple of days a
week.

I had wanted for some time to attend the Women's Community Bible Study, but my job prevented me from being totally involved. A few years ago I began attending the large group when I
was available, but I yearned for more. One spring day I was present
for the final meeting of the year. I had to leave before Communion
was served. I had to hurry home to prepare to go out of town once
more.

As I walked down the steps of the chapel, I was feeling sorry for myself and lamenting the fact that I didn't have time to take a more active part in this wonderful Bible study. And for the first time I can ever recall, God truly spoke to me and said, "You can!" I knew that retirement was somewhere "out there" for me, but my husband had just started a business a few years back, and I'd never considered this a good time for me to give up the security I'd held on to for so long.

You see, from the time my first husband died, I'd always thought I had to provide my own security—I really never considered that I still wasn't letting God take control of my life completely.

But I went home and approached my wonderful and supportive husband with this "off the wall" idea, and except for a few moments of astonishment, he never questioned my decision. I prayed about it constantly—that if it was truly God's will, He would help us. And many situations converged to move me forward in my decision. My church presented me with a significant responsibility, one that I could never accept and still keep my work schedule.

During that summer we saw the movie *The Prince of Egypt,* and when God said to Moses, "If you do my will, I will help you and always be beside you," He was speaking to me again, right there in the Fox Theater!

I joined the Bible study in the fall of 1999 and retired from my career on January 1, 2000. God continues to bless my decision. We continue to be well provided for; our needs are met. Mike's business is flourishing, and I'm finding ways to use my spiritual gifts to serve the Lord more—at church, with a local missions organization, and with my friends and family. I haven't had a moment's regret about retiring.

I wanted to share my story not to encourage you working women to retire, but to let you know that God honors us when we honor Him by trusting Him and doing His will in our lives.

I am blessed daily by learning to step forward and accept His challenges.

He blesses me daily by allowing me to get to know and spend more time with Christian women in Bible study, by giving me more time to listen to Him and study His Word, and by giving me time to prayerfully consider His plan for my life.

Don't be afraid to step forward—His hand is always there to guide you!

Father, thank You for Your guiding companionship in my life and the promise that You will always be with me. Amen.

Joanne Joiner

Many, O Lord my God, are the wonders you have done. The things you planned for us no one can recount to you; were I to speak and tell of them, they would be too many to declare. Psalm 40:5

My Walk with Christ

I realize now that I've always known Christ and that He has always been with me. However, there were years when I questioned His very existence.

Like many Christians, my earliest knowledge of Jesus came from attending Sunday school and learning the song "Jesus Loves Me." However, as a teenager, I began testing the waters and concluded that if Santa Claus wasn't real, then neither was Jesus. In my late teen years, I went through many transitions with no solid foundation, and my faith became contrived. I found myself constantly bargaining with Christ, promising lifestyle changes. While He heard me, I did not hear Him in return.

Eventually, with the support of friends and family, I moved across the country and placed my feet on a new foundation. I met and married a wonderful man, and when our children were born, we returned to the church. My faith was awakening!

When we moved our young family to Atlanta, we joined Peachtree Presbyterian Church, which became an integral part of our lives. We decided to become actively involved in the children's Sunday school program, Wednesday night fellowship dinners, teaching, building Habitat for Humanity houses, and our fabulous adult Sunday school class. My faith was comfortable and growing even more.

Then, nearly ten years ago, a friend invited me to Women's Community Bible Study, which began an entirely new chapter in my life. Every Wednesday from September through April, we met in the chapel for worship through music, followed by an inspiring commentary pertaining to the lesson for that week. Then we divided into smaller groups to discuss in depth how we might be able to apply the weekly lesson to our daily lives. That's when I realized that I *had* to make this Bible study an integral part of my life!

My walk with God became far more personal, as my commitment to Scripture study and prayer drew me ever closer to Him. I cherished this wonderful group of women, aware of the importance of a community of believers coming together each week to worship and glorify God. As the body of Christ, we sought foremost to bring glory to God through His Son, Jesus Christ. (Walking with Him and supporting one another in this endeavor were vital to our faith.)

Over the years, as I met and made friends with many beautiful women at WCBS, I found myself regretting that I hadn't been part of such a group when my children were small. Seeing so many younger mothers faithfully praying for each other's children and spouses caused me to yearn to live the days of raising small children again—only this time walking with Christ *beside* me! I feel certain it would have made a significant difference in the lives of my children as they were growing, changing, and maturing.

God has faithfully grown a tiny Bible study of twelve searching, sometimes doubting, women into a community that encompasses hundreds. For every member who deepens her faith in Christ, His Word is spread tenfold to family, friends, and community. What a beautiful testimony to our love of the Lord Jesus Christ. Now my faith is in Him.

Lord God, thank You for the marvelous ways You bless those who put their faith in You. Amen.

Wendy Kazmarek

*O God, you are my God, earnestly I seek you; my soul thirsts for you,
my body longs for you, in a dry and weary land where there is no
water. I have seen you in the sanctuary and beheld your power and
glory. Because your love is better than life, my lips will glorify you. I
will praise you as long as I live, and in your name I will
lift up my hands. Psalm 63: 1-4*

The Call

It was 1965 and I was 10 years old. In an auditorium of thousands, I was one. You would not have picked me out of a crowd, but God did, and so did Billy Graham. The "call" was issued, and this daring heart picked it up on its radar and began the walk. The Savior was accepted and the Holy Spirit—given at baptism—took flight.

It is not necessary to record the journey of my heart, but it might look familiar to you. For parts of it resemble parts of you. Sometimes my life is so in love with Jesus, it is sure that He is all it needs; and other times circumstances have seduced it to doubt. Sometimes, my heart is a reflection of God's love and mercy; other times, God's reflection blurs and it is human again, imperfect and soiled. Often the day begins in submission to Him; sometimes submission takes a back seat to the illusion of control. Faith is a funny thing. Faith requires letting go of control. It is belief in what you cannot see or feel. And, as faith is the fuel for all believers, it is often what you can see and feel in this life that can devastate the strongest of those.

At no time in my life was this more evident than in the fall of 2000. After many years of leading a small group Bible Study, I decided to take a break, really feeling God's nudge to do so. As I began to slow down and unravel many facets of my life that had been left unattended, I became increasingly vulnerable. Discouragement, isolation and doubt took up residence. It is a dangerous part of our nature to act out of how we feel rather than what we know, and God was working this mighty concept out in my life. For so many years, the wonderful body of believers had nurtured, taught, prayed, and supported me, and I them. But . . . if our liberty in Christ is going to be a reality in life, states author Beth Moore, we are going to have to learn to walk in the freedom of Christ independent of everyone else we know. Like Linus without his blanket, I had purposefully discarded my "busy " life for reflection and contemplation, and the security net of Christian friends for time alone, and I felt utterly unprotected.

There comes a time in every woman's life when an honest assessment becomes necessary, and an honest response can exact a mighty price. Some of us may never honor it, others might dismiss it as insignificant, but there are those courageous hearts that will see it as something too important to deny, and too challenging to fully understand. In the still hours of the day and night, I was forced to come to terms with the weakest part of my personality— trust. Could I trust that God was in the details? Was He there when I and the people I loved made certain choices?

Was He there when I lost my dear friend in college? Or, when I lost my precious grandmother to cancer? Why had I not felt His protection from hurtful friends?

My community of believers had always been there to remind me of two things: God was with me, and things could be worse. But removed from them, I had to do this work alone, and I was failing miserably. I had to turn and face Him with my life. As a deeply intuitive person, I have always been guided by my feelings. How was I to believe without feeling it? A dear counselor likened it to pulling the shade down over a sunny window. The sun was still shining, but my experience of it was that it was not there. The blackout shade had been effective. I found myself at a crossroads. Although I had made a choice at age 10, I was being called in a different way to put my life on the line. I recalled the words of Barbara Brown Taylor about our challenge to faith.

She likened it to a rope bridge swinging out over a gorge. She reminds us that there is often precious little to hang on to except what we have heard to be true: that God promises us that the bridge will hold our weight. And so, in faith, I step out into the uncertainty and untrustworthiness of this world, trusting only in the God who placed His life on the line for me. Yes, I still approach life with passion, but I now approach my faith with discipline. Knowing that praising Him each morning, spending time in His Word, and meeting Him in prayer are where He meets me. And in those dark hours when I cannot seem to feel His presence, I have chosen to believe.

Father God, thank you for the hard lessons learned, for the power to believe in You when I sometimes cannot feel you or see you at work in my life. You have taught me to fuel my passion with spiritual discipline that you might continue your saving work in me.

Kathy Lee

Trust in the LORD with all your heart and lean not on your own understanding; in all your ways acknowledge him and he will make your paths straight. Proverbs 3:5-6

Keeping God in Front

At the age of six, I responded to an altar call at a small neighborhood church. I accepted Jesus as my Savior and can honestly say that I haven't known a day since then when Christ wasn't real in my life. What a blessing! Despite His gracious presence, however, I have experienced many trials and hardships. There have been disappointments, losses, and difficult decisions. He never promised us that the Christian life would be easy!

I joined the Women's Community Bible Study in 1998. Each year's study has been relevant and meaningful, and each small group has been a blessing. I have grown stronger in my walk with Christ and I believe He has used this Bible study to reveal His love for me. Most important, I have learned the simple yet profoundly difficult truth that God has a plan for each of His children, but to accomplish that plan we must let Him have control of our lives.

It is as if we are walking behind God, holding His hand, on a high, narrow road. Suddenly there is a fork in the road, and we stop. Looking down, we see that the road that God is leading us on is full of valleys and swamps and difficult terrain. On the other side of the road lies a beautiful path, smooth and shady. This path looks well traveled. Which way should we go? Should we follow God and stay on the harder, obviously less sensible path? Wouldn't it be much easier to follow the smooth and beautiful trail? Others have.

So often we let go of God's hand and take the easy path. We use our own reasoning and rely on our own abilities. But beyond the bend in the road where we could not see, the road becomes treacherous. God knows what lies beyond our vision, but we do not. If we had followed God through the valleys, we would have come to a place of rest. If we know that we are following God's chosen path for us, even the difficult passages will be a valuable part of the journey. He will not let go of our hand.

It is hard for us to let go and be led. We like to be in control. But God is faithful, and if we are willing, He will take us where He wants us to go. God has a perfect plan for us (Jeremiah 29:11). Christ tells us to rest in Him (Matthew 11:28). We are not to trust our own understanding (Proverbs 3:5) but to let go of anxiety and pray with praise instead (Philippians 4:6). A passage in Psalms urges us to "commit our way to the Lord" (Psalm 37:4-5). It is a daily, sometimes hourly, commitment. We can only stay on His path when we have a strong relationship with Him. Like a child lost in the dark, we need to know the sound of the Father's voice. Once we are willing to let God, through the Holy Spirit, guide our lives, we realize that the difficulty lies not in the journey after all. The difficulty is letting God stay in front.

Father, help me to continue to let go and trust You to guide my life for Your glory. Amen.

Pam Martin

*"Seek ye first the kingdom of God
and his righteousness." (Matthew 6:33)*

*Christ at
the Center*

When my husband and I were starting our family life in Atlanta, we were trying to be responsible, respectable, and of course, religious. We were a young couple eager to do what was right in relation to children, community, career, and of course, church. But all that changed on a sultry summer night in 1985.

Terry was out of town on business and I had just put our two babies in bed for the night. Exhausted as usual, I plopped down in front of the television to be entertained for a moment when I came across a "TV preacher" who captured my attention. I stopped for a moment, fully intending to continue my channel surfing—but I couldn't. He had me—or should I say God had me—and before I knew it I was on my knees crying and praying for forgiveness.

What, you might ask, was he preaching about? Based on what I've told you already, you won't be surprised to learn it wasn't adultery, partying, immorality, stealing, or cheating that I was repenting of. It was something far more life-threatening: making myself the center of my life and leaving Jesus Christ on the outside. The preacher was asking a question in his message that cut me to the quick: "Is Jesus Christ the center of your life?" My first reaction was that I didn't know what he was talking about—which meant my answer had to be, "No."

I couldn't switch the channel because I wanted to know what it meant to make Christ the center of my life. If his question had been, "Are you a Christian?" I would have answered "Yes." I had accepted Christ as my Savior as a teenager, and I felt that when I died I would go to heaven. But beyond providing a way for me to gain eternal life, Christ had never become a meaningful part of my life. In fact, I didn't realize He had a role to play at all. There was no doubt I had been living my life with me at the center.

As the preacher continued, he explained that when we invite Jesus into our life, it's very much like getting married. We take our vows and the honeymoon might be great, but if there is not a daily commitment to communicate and to get to know your partner, the relationship can grow stale and two people can easily grow apart. Of course, in the case of a relationship with God, the only person growing apart was me, not God.

He explained that WE have a part in seeking after God. (Jeremiah 29:13 says, "You will seek me and find me when you seek me with all your heart.") He also explained that God is always reaching out to us and is there to help us—if we draw near to Him, He will draw near to us. He said God had a special plan for each of our lives that He reveals as we come to know Him. But we need to put Him in charge of each day. By turning to Him daily for guidance, forgiveness, and love, we begin to put Him (instead of ourselves) at the center of our lives. While this is a gradual process, the result is a life full of love, meaning, and purpose as never before.

I knew as I sat and listened to the preacher that I had been missing out on the most important relationship of my life. For some reason, I never really knew that the almighty living God wanted to have a relationship with a person like me.

After a deeply heartfelt prayer asking Christ to become the center of my life—and asking Him to help me do what it takes to make that happen—I fell into bed. The next day's mail brought an invitation to a neighborhood Bible study (how does God time these things so perfectly?) which I accepted—in spite of the fact that I wasn't even sure what a Bible study was. I called a couple of friends to go with me so I wouldn't be alone, and the rest, as they say, is history. God set me on a path that gets clearer every day—learning to live with Christ at the center of my life. He has filled an emptiness and a loneliness that I never really knew I had before. He has supplied joy with every daily challenge, and provided peace in every circumstance as I learn to rest in His sovereign care.

Bible studies introduced me to God's Word and I spent several years devouring every book and hounding every teacher I could find. I was like a person who hadn't eaten a meal for years suddenly being invited to a banquet. I was eventually asked to teach a small group of women at my church, a study which has grown into the Women's Community Bible Study of Atlanta—a family of dear sisters in Christ. Today my husband edits my commentaries, and our four teenagers are leading other kids in Bible study. I am so thankful God got my attention through a TV preacher nearly two decades ago.

To be responsible, respectable, and religious is not bad—but being those things doesn't lead to knowing God. Life is not about us. Life is about God. And the Christian life is not about what we can do for Him, but more about what He has already done for us. When we understand this, our service to Him is one of gratitude and joy. In order to have a personal relationship with Jesus Christ, we must spend daily time getting to know Him. For to know Him is to love Him, and with Him we find life as it was meant to be lived.

Dear Heavenly Father, how can I ever thank you for changing my life?!! You have touched my heart with the importance of putting Christ first. With your help, I can live my life for Him. All praises to You forever!

Nancy McGuirk

There is a time for everything, and a season for every activity under heaven. Ecclesiastes 3:1

"But I Just Don't Have Enough Time!"

Having grown up in a Catholic family and educated in a Catholic elementary school (which meant daily Mass before school), I definitely fit the mold of the commonly used term *cradle Catholic*. In middle and high school, I attended a non-Catholic school, but I attended mandatory religion classes after Mass on Sundays. Knowing this background, you would think I would know more about the Bible, but my biblical knowledge was extremely lacking. I had never heard of a Bible study at my church or in my school but felt my needs were met with the Scripture readings during Mass.

In 1995, I attended our Catholic school's mothers' retreat, where we were challenged to consider joining a women's Bible study. Bible studies were not particularly plentiful in Catholic churches, so I elbowed my sister, who was seated next to me, and suggested we join Women's Community Bible Study in the fall. What a wonderful decision it was, and we've both continued to participate. Unlike attending Mass, which I confess (remember, I'm Catholic!) can become somewhat routine, WCBS was very inspiring, thought-provoking, and interactive. I had always been told never to talk about religion or politics outside the family, but in this study I found an open forum for even my most challenging scriptural concerns. At first, I was fairly reserved (highly unusual for me), absorbing all the discussion and sharing little. Over time, I have realized that I need to express my thoughts because so often others struggle with similar concerns.

Tennis, golf, daily walks, and volunteer activities were all important to me during my free time while my children were at school. Initially, attending Bible study was a struggle for me to fit into my self-inflicted, time-crunched routine. *Maybe I don't have enough time for this,* I thought. *I'll put it off until my two children are in college.* What initially seemed an inconvenience has now become top priority. I no longer begrudge the time my class preparation takes but instead look forward to it, setting my alarm clock early each morning. I feel as though God is waiting for me in my family room to reflect on His Word, and I wouldn't want to disappoint Him. The inner peace I have always felt I had has truly been magnified. Now I am actually familiar with our Sunday Mass Scripture readings because I've studied them weekly. The enthusiasm I have gained from the Bible study has spilled over to my family. My husband, John, joined a men's Bible study; and my children, who both attend a Catholic school, come to me with questions from their religion classes. Before participating regularly in Bible study, I would not have been comfortable navigating through the Bible with them. Their questions have generated some interesting discussions. What could I possibly do that would have more meaning to my family than to spark an interest in such a treasured book?

After I learned an acronym for BIBLE—"Basic Instructions Before Leaving Earth"—I realized the importance of daily, not just weekly, readings of Scripture. After all, I seemed to fit my other activities in my schedule more than once a week! Prioritizing is something I am constantly trying to do in my daily life. I have found that my Bible study has gone from last to first place in priority and that studying the Bible, along with the Christian fellowship I enjoy each week, is more fulfilling than any tennis match or round of golf I have played!

I thank God for the challenge made to me six years ago. Because of WCBS, my priorities have definitely been put on a more eternal course. The daily patience, understanding, and gratitude I feel for my family and friends have grown exponentially. For those of you reading this testimony who are not currently participating in a Scripture study, consider this challenge. I dare say it will be the most beneficial two hours you will spend all week—for yourself and for those you may encounter in your daily life.

Dear God, thank You for the rich blessings of my life, for Your guiding presence and Your deep and unconditional love. Help me to stay Christ-centered rather than focused on the things of this world, resting in the knowledge that there is a time for everything and a season for every activity under heaven. Amen.

Toni Rhett

One thing I ask of the Lord, this is what I seek: that I may dwell in the house of the Lord all the days of my life, to gaze upon the beauty of the Lord, and to seek him in his temple. Psalm 27:4

His Good and Perfect Will

When I was a junior in college, I went through a valley of sorts—not only questioning doctrinal teachings but also wondering if I had any faith at all. Worse yet, I wasn't sure whether God even existed. Is God who He says He is, and can He do what He says He can? I wrestled continually with my questioning, doubting spirit. Ultimately, my search for God's intervention and guidance opened doors for me that I never could have imagined possible. I came to realize that Jesus was indeed real and alive, and He called me to make a personal commitment of faith. Through God's grace I was able to comprehend that God has always been present in the details of my life, faithfully revealing Himself whenever I truly sought His face. I became deeply aware of the fact that He has been a constant source of peace in an ever-changing world because His character is unchanging (Malachi 3:6). While I may be prone to wander, particularly in my less stressful times, my Father never wanders from me. The real miracle is that during my most challenging times, Jesus has graced me with the faith and courage to press on (Isaiah 46:4).

My relationship with Jesus has given me the freedom to make life-changing decisions. Knowing that He is in control and will work in my life even when I make mistakes is such a comfort! Inevitably, He uses my mistakes in order to work them to fulfill His good and perfect will (Proverbs 19:21). He considers my

"Martha" nature, which keeps me in such a busy, hurried state, contrary to the way Jesus intends for us to live, and teaches me many lessons in how to be quiet (Psalm 46:10). I seem to continually struggle with remaining at rest and having a gentle and quiet spirit, yet His steady presence in my life continues to fortify me (1 Peter 3:4).

I have developed many friendships through Women's Community Bible Study over the years. I believe that the true bonds of our sisterhood will last not only through this lifetime but for eternity. I have been blessed beyond measure by so many of these women who were willing, at a moment's notice, to clear their schedules in order to meet and pray with someone in need. We have been awed by the miraculous way in which God has worked in our relatively small community: healing broken marriages, those afflicted with cancer, clinical depression, and many other devastating conditions. These truly are God's miracles today! We pray for His will in people's lives to result in His glorification. First John 3:18 says, "Let us not love with words or tongue, but with actions and in truth." WCBS has provided the opportunity to grow in my relationship with Jesus, and at the same time, to be a servant for Him.

Father, keep me focused on Your presence in my life that I may dwell in Your house forever. Amen.

Jeannie Ross

*It is better to take refuge in the LORD than to trust in man. Psalm 118:8
Confess your sins to each other and pray for each other so that you
may be healed. The prayer of a righteous man is powerful
and effective. James 5:16*

My Refuge in Christ

It is with awesome wonder that I begin to write my testimony. My walk with Christ has been a journey with temptations, trials, adversity, and joy. At the age of twelve, I accepted Christ as my Savior in my small country church in Tennessee. I had the privilege of a loving family and friends to support me when it came to issues of faith. While I knew Christ loved me unconditionally, I guess those early years were more about religion, fear of doing wrong, and following the golden rule than establishing a true relationship with Christ. Imagine being the oldest child and wanting to be perfect in everything, not realizing the pressure and insidious nature that such a goal can wreak. While surrounded by love and the best of intentions, I soon realized how God gives us free will to make decisions. If we are not in relationship with Him and if we don't really pray for discernment, we can get ourselves into a heap of trouble quickly. I began pretending that everything was okay when in reality I was about to lose it. As an article my grandmother gave me in college stated, I had developed a Type E personality, trying to be all things to all people. It never occurred to me that the world always asks more of you than you can do. Unfortunately, my innocence and lack of ability to say no landed me in a date rape situation in college, and I began shutting down emotionally. I prayed for guidance but never quite understood the true meaning of faith: total reliance on God and willingness to do His will. I became emotionally sick and, as a registered dietitian, I knew I was approaching eating disorder status because I tried to control my life instead of letting God. My repressed emotion reared itself again after I lost my first pregnancy (a tubal pregnancy). I thought my choices were haunting me. I believed God was punishing me. Luckily, I did conceive, had a healthy child, loving husband, and a blessed life.

Then a combination of circumstances took me into the darkest time of my life. I developed a postpartum anxiety and depression that led to two four-month periods that were literally hell on earth. Every day was a temptation to choose life or death. Self-destructive, suicidal thoughts barely scratch the surface of what was going on in my mind. The devil's oppression was real and surreal. Psalm 23:4—"Even though I walk through the valley of the shadow of death, I will fear no evil, for you are with me; your rod and your staff, they comfort me"—became words I clung to and repeated. God was my tether when I had nothing left to hold on to. I had to let go and allow God to be God. While in psychiatric outpatient and inpatient programs, I learned you are only as sick as your secrets. Because of my perfectionism, Type E personality, and desire for control, I had nearly self-destructed. Additionally, the medications I was given made my condition even worse. During this time, prayer by myself and by others was more powerful than I ever knew. Bible studies and healing services kept me surrounded with Christ's love. In Ephesians 6, I read voraciously about the armor of God. This was spiritual battle, and I needed every weapon to resist the devil's attacks. I was healed and knew God was transforming my life. Genesis 50:24 states that what was meant for evil and destruction, God can use for good. I learned that tears of pain, sorrow, and despair can become tears of comfort and joy when we know that He is in control and that we are more precious to God than anything. Not only was I positively changed, but so was everyone close to me, including my husband, child, parents, siblings, in-laws, extended family, and friends. Their steadfastness in prayer and faith in God grew. Prayer is powerful, and hearing God's Word helps faith grow. Glorifying God in my life is my priority now. I am humbled by His love for me. When it comes to praising Him, I am like the Energizer bunny—I keep going and going and going.

Dear Father, You are my refuge and shield. Your strength and protection cover me, and I entrust my emotional well-being to Your care. Make my life accountable to You and my heart open to confession so that I may pray for the healing of others. You are faithful to Your promises that the prayers of the righteous are powerful and effective. In Christ's holy name I pray, Amen.

Elizabeth Cowan Thomason

*Being confident of this, that he who began a good work in you will
carry it on to completion until the day of Christ Jesus. Philippians 1:6*

The Slow Drip

There is nothing more powerful than hearing someone give
their testimony and tell about a tough experience God carried them
through. God is always glorified in these stories, and the person
giving the testimony always seems to be strengthened in their faith.
My story is nothing like that, however. For me, life is good and
God is good! For God has taken more of a "slow drip" approach
with me.

As a child, I always went to church. There was never any discussion about whether or not we would go. We always went. Later,
as a young adult, I attended a small woman's Christian college and
can remember being very touched as we nightly sang the Doxol-
ogy in the gorgeous dining room. However, I do not ever remember any dramatic, life changing experience with my Savior.

It is only now, as an adult, that I have finally begun to recog-
nize that God has been at work in my life all along. It has been a
"slow drip," but I know I have been fundamentally changed through
the years. At some point, I crossed the line and claimed Christ as
my Lord and Savior. I don't know when. I just know it happened.

Several years ago, I was invited to attend WCBS. I turned down
the opportunity initially because it conflicted with my aerobics
schedule. Little did I know how much more "fit" I would be if I
had attended. When I finally did accept the invitation to come, I
attended regularly but rarely did the homework. It took a couple
of years to figure out that God desires me to do my part in the
relationship with Him!

I will never forget sitting in the chapel one morning and hearing our speaker say, "If you want to hear God laugh, tell Him what *your* plans are!" I laughed with everyone else and thought about my plans and how I knew exactly what God had in store for me. Little did I know that God was chuckling with what *He* had planned. That very evening, my husband announced that we were putting our house on the market and moving to Madison, a small town in Georgia. Within one week, our house had sold. We made an easy move to Madison. It was obvious that God had plans for us!

After several years of traveling from Madison to Atlanta for Bible study, God called me and another friend to begin our own WCBS satellite in my home. Every Monday, God gives us the gift of turning my den into a sanctuary for Him. I am still growing and still struggling and very grateful each time God makes another "slow drip" into my life with Him. I am sure that He has more plans for me and that He will continue the work He has started.

Lord, may I be reminded every day that You are continually at work in my life. I have no need to fear what each day may bring for You are in control.

Anne Trulock

THREE

When God Changes You . . .

You Are Comforted Through Loss

Praise be to the God and Father of our Lord Jesus Christ,
the Father of compassion and the God of all comfort,
who comforts us in all our troubles,
so that we can comfort those in any trouble
with the comfort we ourselves have received from God.
2 Corinthians 1:3-4

Do you know anyone who hasn't suffered some kind of loss? Even if you didn't know anyone besides yourself, that would be enough. Your own tears have been sufficient to teach you that life is filled with loss.

Our minds go first to those most painful losses—perhaps a spouse through death or divorce, perhaps the untimely loss of a child, perhaps a parent or a beloved friend. But there is more to every loss than what is immediately apparent. Think of the loss of a marriage relationship. It certainly involves the loss of a partner, but it is also the loss of dreams, desires, intimacy, security, and the possibility of growing old with a best friend. With every visible loss there are a host of invisible ones that multiply the pain beyond any imagining. And it is not a matter of if we will suffer loss in this life—only a matter of when. Many people dread life's losses because they fear not having the resources for coping. And it is a very real fear. Losses can debilitate some who seemed so strong.

The greatest resource at a time of loss is comfort—the presence of another person who will walk down a dark path with us. And yet, there is a hierarchy of those who can comfort us. A complete stranger can help, but a friend who has had a similar experience is even better. Or perhaps a person who can give us advice and direction when we seem immobilized by pain will help. But ultimately, there is one person who can comfort us beyond all others, and that is God Himself. Think of what He has lost—the paradise He created for us to live in, the sinless relationship with His first two children, the loyalty of many through the years who professed to love Him but turned their backs on Him, and ultimately His own Son to the cruelty of a Roman cross. No one knows loss better than God.

Following are stories by women who suffered loss and who found ultimate comfort in God Himself.

If we confess our sins, He is faithful and just
to forgive us our sins. 1 John 1:9

A Forgiving God

Several years ago, I was at my doctor's office for the four-month visit in my pregnancy. When the ultrasound picture appeared, we saw the most precious little baby, lying on its back, sucking its tiny thumb. In our excitement, we didn't notice the doctor's face. Something was wrong. Upon closer examination of the screen and the sound monitor, no movement was detected. The doctor turned off the machine and quickly delivered the words I will never forget: "I'm sorry. There seems to have been a miscarriage. The baby did not survive."

For most people the sadness would have been shocking, overwhelming, devastating. But I realized instantly how God must feel when He loses a wanted child. You see, a few years before this miscarriage, I had an abortion because I became pregnant before I was married. As much as I hate to admit it, I never even considered giving birth. I didn't think of the baby at all; I thought only of my family, my image, my mother's reaction. I never considered any option besides abortion.

Now, I know I cannot blame the way I was raised or anyone else for my actions. I was living so far out of God's plan for me, I didn't even bother to try to discover what His plan was for me. I just wanted to wipe away this bad situation as if it never happened.

That day in the parking garage of the doctor's office, after I had been told that my baby had died, I asked God to forgive me. I felt His presence as never before. I believe I heard Him saying to me, "Child, I am on your side, and I did not want you to lose that baby."

The Lord has since opened my heart and sent the Holy Spirit in to free me. My sorrow is real, though, and I still need your prayers to be able to forgive myself. Rarely does a day go by that I don't wonder what my baby would look and act like, how I would feel when he or she laughed, what grade he or she would be in every single year.

Can God forgive even someone like me? He certainly has. He has cleared my future for me so that I can move forward in peace. Jesus Christ is always with me, and He loves me in spite of everything I've done. He is the best friend I have ever known.

Lord, we confess our sins, believing in faith that You will forgive us. May we be assured of Your incredible mercy so that we may confess even the most painful sins in our lives.

Anonymous

*Trust in the LORD with all your heart and lean
understanding; in all your ways acknowledge hi*
your paths straight. Proverbs 3:

A Guiding Trust

I grew up going to Sunday school and church. My mother never missed a revival, and neither did her five children. I never remember a time in my life when I didn't believe in Jesus. I would later learn the difference between believing and fearing God versus knowing and truly trusting Him. But those scriptures I had memorized in my early Sunday school years came to my mind just when I needed something to hold on to the most.

Within a few days of the 1986 space shuttle explosion, my big brother called to let me know that my mother had been hospitalized. Several years before, she had been diagnosed with rheumatoid arthritis, and her health had steadily declined. I now cherish this phone call, as it turned out to be the last time I heard my brother's voice. One month later, when I was twenty-nine, my big brother, only thirty-four, lost his life in a horrible accident. He was a husband, a father to two small children, a brother, and a son. We were a close-knit family, and his tragic death simply devastated us all. The only comfort we could find in this situation was knowing that he was a Christian and that he went to heaven.

Six months after this devastating event, my family as I knew it began to unravel. Revelations occurred that eventually led my parents to divorce after forty-two years of marriage. I was thirty-four, had a young child of my own, and felt like a broken little girl. How could all these things happen to a "Christian" family?

I prayed so much for my mother's health. Why wouldn't God

her? She loved God more than anyone I knew. She of all people did not deserve this physical pain too. More than anyone, my mom taught me to trust in the Lord. She never lost her faith in God. She prayed for her family and for anyone who was even a little blue. Her love for Christ and compassion for others while in a state of total dependence were her miracle to her broken family. If she could believe and love God that much, how could I question His sovereignty? How could my search for truth lead anywhere but to her Savior, Jesus Christ? She is now in heaven, but the way she lived her life continues to guide lives here on earth.

Six years ago a friend of mine invited me to attend a women's Bible study at her church. Up to that point, I would have said that God was first in my life, and in some intellectual way, He was; but as I began to study His Word and spend deliberate time with Him, He became first in my *heart*. In the process of putting Him in His proper place, He began to heal the brokenness and hurt in my life. No one could do this for me except my gentlemanly heavenly Father who waited for my permission to do so.

God did not want me just to believe in Him; He wanted me to *know* Him by spending time with Him. He wanted me to understand His words by personally guiding and showing me what He meant by them. He wanted me whole, not broken; free, not bound. My trust in Him is deeper and more personal as I surrender to His will. I often fail to surrender daily, but thankfully, "His compassions never fail. They are new every morning; great is His faithfulness" (Lamentations 3:22-23).

Heavenly Father, though often I do not understand Your plans, You have always been faithful in leading me in ways that increase my faith in You. Thank You!

Lynn Stanton Adams

How, then, can they call on the one they have not believed in? And how can they believe in the one of whom they have not heard? And how can they hear without someone preaching to them? Romans 10:14

Time Out
for the Unexpected

Two weeks after Easter, in April 1998, my family had to face the "C" word. My father had just been diagnosed with advanced cancer. My first thought was, *This is it. What is going to happen to my precious father?* I worried. Panic set in.

Cancer was trying to steal my father, and I was unsure what would happen to him when he died. He demonstrated Christian qualities, but we had certainly never discussed his relationship with Jesus. I felt burdened to help my father understand what God had done and was doing in my life.

I'm not sure what my husband and children did that summer, as I spent only six days in Atlanta. But I know the Holy Spirit was at work, and I felt the Spirit urging me to talk to Daddy about Christ.

Romans 10:14 asks, "How can they hear without someone preaching to them?" Finally one day I woke Daddy from a nap, asked him to listen to a tape I had brought, warned him that it was real strong, and said that we'd talk afterward. The tape contained the testimony of a successful businessman who had come to know Christ after he received a diagnosis similar to my father's. Daddy lay there with his head buried in his pillow, holding my hand. If anything, I recognized that getting the message through to him was a long shot. But after he heard the tape, he said it was fantastic. Thinking of Romans 10:14, I asked him to repeat a prayer after me: "Heavenly Father, I ask You to come into my life today. Help me gain strength and feel strength in You."

From that day on, I read to Daddy every day from the Bible. Spending this time with him proved to be very beneficial. It helped me cope with my fear of losing my father. It also greatly comforted me to know that God was working in him, and I could see a sense of peace in him—the peace that passes all understanding. Daddy even began asking me to read to him more often.

In my quiet time with God, I pleaded to be able to be with my father until the end. I begged God not to take him until Daddy was ready for Him. A little less than three weeks before his death, my father wrote me a note saying that his future was in God's hands and he couldn't feel more comfortable. I will treasure this note forever.

On August 19, 1998, a few minutes before my father's last breath, my mother prayed aloud, thanking God for bringing Dad into her life. She thanked God for the wonderful father he had been to his three children and for Dad's being a good and faithful servant. Moments later, my father was in the Holy Spirit's hands and in the presence of our heavenly Father.

Dear Lord, I am deeply grateful for Your love and abiding presence in my life. Fill me with Your Holy Spirit and help me share the news of Your saving grace with people who do not have a personal relationship with You. Make me bold for You, Father, that I might glorify Your name. Amen.

Sully Beckham

We know that in everything God works for good with those who love
Him, who are called according to His purpose. Romans 8:28

Why, God, Why?

I knew how blessed I was—really I did. I had three beautiful children, a wonderful husband who had just accepted an exciting and challenging new job, and a life full of family, friends, and activities. Then my life crashed. Less than three weeks after being diagnosed with leukemia, my two-year-old son, Brian, died. To say that I was crushed doesn't even begin to touch the surface. My life stopped. While I struggled with why I had even been left here on this earth, friends cooked meals for my family, did the grocery shopping, took my other children to various activities, and listened to me cry out in despair: "Why, God, why?"

No answer made sense to me. "Why?" continues to be my most difficult question. I believe with all my heart that God could have saved Brian from cancer, but He chose not to perform that miracle. In the six years that have passed since Brian's death, I have learned through prayer and reading and studying God's Word to put aside the question and just trust in His infinite wisdom. His plan is simply beyond my comprehension, and making that "leap of faith" has finally allowed me some peace.

Every step of the way God has been with me, placing strong Christian women in my path to guide me. Someone invited me to Women's Community Bible Study at the very lowest point in my life. I was placed in a group whose leader, now my very dear friend, had also lost a child. Other Bible study members gently encouraged me to question and define my beliefs. Whenever I lost strength, I received a card in the mailbox, an invitation to lunch, a shoulder to cry on, or just a smile and a hug. I know that God placed people in this group to see me through. I thank Him for that, and I pray that as

I grow strong, He will use me to help others through their dark times.

I have come a long way since my first Bible study meeting. That day I could hardly see through my own tears, but I knew that I was in a safe place; I was where I was meant to be. In the commentaries and in the small-group meetings, each woman hears the message God wants her to hear. Familiar words take on new meaning as God whispers His desires to each of us. He speaks clearly in the presence of believers, if we learn to listen. Over the past few years, God's Word has revealed three life-changing truths to me.

1. *Romans 8:28 says, "We know that in everything God works for good with those who love Him, who are called according to His purpose."* This verse does not mean that everything in this world is good, but that God will bring good things from all that happens.

2. *John 3:16 tells us, "God so loved the world that He gave his only Son, that whoever believes in Him should not perish but have eternal life."* I can only begin to feel God's pain at the torturous treatment and death of His own Son. Yet, He allowed it to happen to save me and to save you. His plan is so much greater than we can even imagine.

3. *Hebrews 11:1 reminds us, "Now faith is the assurance of things hoped for, the conviction of things not seen."* I cannot see God, but I can see His handiwork, His disciples, and the love of His people. I know that He is with me.

I still have a long way to go in my journey with Christ. I feel very fortunate to be part of such a positive force in the body of WCBS. Jesus said, "For where two or three are gathered in my name, there I am in the midst of them" (Matthew 18:20). He *is* here. Just listen for His whisper.

Dear Lord, thank You for being with us through all of life's circumstances. Help us hear Your whisper of love even in the midst of our pain.

Lynn Ceto

Peace I leave with you, my peace I give unto you: not as the world giveth, give I unto you. Let not your heart be troubled, neither let it be afraid. John 14:27 (KJV)

Are You There, God? It's Me, Nancy

Have you ever experienced inner peace during a time in your life when you felt totally broken? With God, such peace is possible. After my husband, Steve, and I lost our daughter, Emily, to Sudden Infant Death Syndrome, I was wrought with grief. Up until this point, my life had been smooth sailing: I grew up in a loving home, attended excellent schools, had dear friendships, met and married a wonderful man, and was grateful to be a stay-at-home mother to our two healthy and beautiful daughters.

On the morning of August 15, 1996, a silent killer took the life of my precious three-month-old daughter during her nap. In the days and weeks following her death, I went to the cemetery, sat by her grave, and pondered how and why something so terrible could happen to my baby girl and our family. Even though our friends and family members showered us with love, I still felt total despair and loneliness. I felt out of control and helpless. I kept asking myself what I might have done differently to keep this nightmare from happening. I was Emily's mother, and my responsibility was to care for her and protect her—yet there was nothing I could do. She was gone, and I was left to deal with my grief.

I have always considered myself a Christian: I grew up going to church and Sunday school, went through confirmation, participated in the church youth program, and often prayed to God. Yet I wondered where He was through all of this. How could a loving

God allow my baby to die? Had I come to a crossroads in my faith journey? I knew God as my Savior; he had granted me salvation. However, I needed something more from Him. I needed to be assured that His presence was real.

As I sat at the cemetery one afternoon, I offered myself two options: to look to Him for comfort and guidance or to shut Him out completely. I chose to cry out to God for help, and that day, on the grassy hill overlooking the lake, He made His presence known to me in a very real way. He comforted me and restored my soul. I knew in my heart He was saying that He could truly feel my pain, for He too lost a child and knew a parent's grief. He filled me with an inner peace that I didn't know I could feel. He was so alive to me, and this experience opened my eyes and heart to a real and living Father. No longer was God just an abstract thought; He became my Everlasting Father, my Prince of Peace.

I left the cemetery that day still grief-stricken over my loss, but I didn't feel so alone anymore. I knew I wasn't alone, and I had never been alone. God was just patiently waiting for me to call out to Him. Thus began a beautiful journey, one I will continue for the rest of my life. Even though life continues to present hard times, I know that I am never alone. I am blessed to be a child of God filled with hope and peace.

Everlasting Father, in our moments of despair, send us Your peace to calm our fears and soothe our hearts.

Nancy Fallon

"For I know the plans I have for you," declares the LORD, *"plans to prosper you and not to harm you, plans to give you hope and a future." Jeremiah 29:11*

God's Plan for My Life

Through personal heartbreak and happiness, I have found God to be steadfast, faithful, and always present. In the midst of very difficult circumstances, God has given me not only the strength to move forward but also a greater understanding of His grace and power. I am confident that God will never leave me or forsake me.

As young adults, my husband, Peter, and I lost our firstborn child due to a congenital heart defect. We were devastated and turned to God, but we truly did not understand Jesus' power to comfort us. Neither of us had ever truly suffered hardship, but as we grew closer as a couple, we grew closer to God. For the first time in our lives, we understood that we were powerless to make a difference. We had turned to God for comfort but did not know the truth of Jeremiah 29:11, that God has a plan to prosper you and give you a future and a hope.

Ten years later, Peter was diagnosed with an inoperable, fatal type of cancer, and was given six weeks to live. Without any hope we turned to God for a plan, comfort, and strength. Through the guidance of my senior pastor and many doctors, we developed a plan that miraculously provided both a future and a hope. While struggling through many surgeries and medical roadblocks, Peter lived for ten years. God's presence and comfort were very real to us.

When Peter was first diagnosed with cancer, our children were ages one, three, and five. Peter often said that he wanted to live long enough for his children to know and remember him. During those ten years, God and family were our two top priorities. As a family we relied on God through prayer to sustain us day by day. Through those trying times, we felt God's grace in the midst of very difficult days. The peace that passes all understanding was made clear to us.

Since his death nine years ago, all three children have thrived and do remember their dad well! I have learned that God will never forsake me and will always be present when I seek Him. God's plan for me is far better than any one I can dream of or orchestrate. My responsibility is to seek God's plan for my life through prayer and to always keep my eyes on Him. I must be faithful and wait upon God's timing because I know He is always there for me. Often I need to remember what God says in Psalm 46: "Be still and know that I am God." I am not always patient, but I do know that God's plan for my life is perfect.

Father God, thank You for Your plan for my life, a plan with a future and a hope and the assurance of a perfect eternity with You. Amen.

Marie Hoffman

I am sure that neither death nor life nor things present, nor things to come, nor anything else in all creation, will be able to separate us from the love of God in Christ Jesus our Lord. Romans 8:38

A Broken Heart
Made Whole

In 1990, when I was asked to join the Bible study (which eventually became Women's Community Bible Study), I was at an all-time high. Happily married, I was the proud mother of a four-year-old daughter and finally was pregnant with a healthy baby after having suffered two miscarriages. I was vitally in love with the Lord for blessing me so! It was such a special time in my life, as this new group of Christian women enveloped me, showering my precious unborn child with love and prayers each week we met.

Three months later, what appeared to be a routine labor and delivery tragically left my beloved baby daughter, Carey, brain-dead. She survived for twelve devastating weeks.

Carey's loss was compounded by the untimely deaths of my parents in an automobile accident seven years earlier. My grief and anger were truly beyond measure. My faith was under the ultimate fire, not only because of losing our child, but because of the tragic deaths of my mother and father, whose love and support I so dearly missed during this terrible period of my life. The Lord, whom I had praised only months before, became the target of my bitter and angry soul. I dropped out of the Bible study and isolated myself from the world, my deep wounds causing my heart to become harder and harder. There seemed to be no hope.

But in spite of my blasphemous and venomous ways, the "relentless Hound of heaven" would not leave me alone in my miseries. The twelve women in the Bible study extended Christ's love to me and prayed for me until I was able to live again. When Christ commanded His disciples to love others as He had loved them, He was not talking about people who were easy to love! This tenacious group of women had their work cut out for them, yet they never gave up on me.

In the sorrow-filled months that followed, I came to a whole new understanding of God. I realized that I had received grace in its finest hour. Grace—that infusion of strength and blessing when you least expect and deserve it. I came to understand unconditional love because I experienced genuine love in spite of myself and my actions. And ultimately, I realized that God works in profoundly mysterious ways. On many days when I felt that I could not put one foot in front of the other, loving acts of kindness would appear at my door. Meals, flowers, and encouraging notes all demonstrated God's transforming power of unconditional love for His bereaved children.

As I write this testimony, I am three days away from my sweet Carey's eleventh birthday. I can't help but reflect on her smiling down upon her once "lost" mother who now through grace alone can minister to others who have lost children or parents and desperately need to renew their hope in the Lord. I am again in love with my Lord—for good this time, because now I understand His character.

Dear Lord, I thank You every day for our Women's Community Bible Study as it continues to fuel and renew me with His truths.

Linda Wyatt

FOUR

When God Changes You . . .

You Are Lifted During Difficult Times

*And we know that in all things God works for the good
of those who love him, who have been
called according to his purpose. Romans 8:28*

Out of the six interrogatives we use every day—Who? What? When? Where? Why? How?—surely the most asked is "Why?" We overused that question when we were two, and now our own children direct it at us at the slightest bit of dissatisfaction with our parental decisions. It's not a bad question—in fact, it's a highly reasonable one. Something in us assumes an orderly explanation exists for every action and reaction in this world.

Our inclination to ask "Why?" is put there by God. But it gets frustrated when we ask it of mortals who don't always have a good answer—specifically parents, teachers, coaches, good friends, or anybody else we think has put an obstacle in our path. But those people don't always know why they do or say what they do. The best answer we might get from a friend is, "I don't know—

just because!" Or the classic answer that comes from an authority figure is, "Because I said so!" Our parents and teachers were often so busy trying to maintain calm and control that they pulled rank when they didn't have a well-reasoned answer to our whys.

But we have to uncondition ourselves from that frustration when we ask God, "Why?" He always knows the answer to the question, unlike our friends who may not know. Neither does He pull rank because He's tired or angry or doesn't have time to deal with us. God knows the answer to every "Why" question we ask during difficult times in our lives. We can avoid frustration during hard times by trusting God, by believing His plans and purposes are there. We should never take His decision not to answer us specifically as evidence that He lacks a good reason. Instead, we should take comfort in knowing that God is never arbitrary or capricious, tired or too busy, baffled or amazed by what happens in our lives.

This section contains stories of women who had questions for God and who learned to take comfort in the fact that everything in life fits somewhere into God's plans.

Thanks be to God, who always leads us in His triumph in Christ and manifests through us the sweet aroma of Him. 2 Corinthians 2:14

A Fragrant Aroma

Nine years ago I was handed a "cup of horror." That is what King David called desperate times in Psalm 60:3. Until then I had not experienced personally such "cups" in life.

A cup of horror is a time in life when our kind and gracious God allows His child to experience heartbreaking pain or struggle. During the experience, your faith is shaken and you wonder: How could God allow this to happen to me? For example, how could a good and loving God allow a terminal illness? How could my child be on drugs? How could my Christian marriage break up?

Even though I was a born-again Christian, for over a year I focused mainly on the pain. I was angry with God. Then God broke through with this verse: "God's favor is on those who search for good" (Proverbs 11:27). I certainly needed and wanted His favor. I certainly had not been searching for good. "How can I focus on good?" I asked.

God led me to start a journal and include in each entry five good things that had happened that day. My entries were as simple as listening to the wood thrush in the morning. They were as exciting as planning vacation trips. The journal changed my life. It removed the focus on my pain.

A second life-changing event occurred a couple of years later, when a friend asked me to go with her to Women's Community Bible Study. I had participated in Bible studies before, even led them. This Bible study was different from others I had attended because it emphasized worshiping and praising God. Precious women came together every week and focused on the many blessings Christ had given them. They spoke of their Friend and the Lover of their souls. They were filled with love for others. As Ephesians 5:2 says, "Be full of love for others, following the example of Christ who loved you and gave Himself to God as a sacrifice to take away your sins. And God was pleased, for Christ's love for you was like sweet perfume to Him."

Do I still have my "cup"? Yes. But the aroma is different as I carry it. "Thanks be to God, who always leads us in His triumph in Christ and manifests through us the sweet aroma of the knowledge of Him in every place" (2 Corinthians 2:14).

Loving God, help us always to search for good. Fill us with love for others so that we may spread the sweet fragrance of Christ's love with those around us.

Anonymous

Ask and it will be given to you; seek and you will find; knock and the door will be opened to you. Matthew 7:7

Like Learning to Ice Skate at Fifty

My journey with God began years ago, when I was diagnosed with stage II breast cancer. Rather than reacting with fear, I responded with self-inflicting guilt. I told myself, "I've let down my husband, my kids, *everyone*. No one can take care of them except me." I did not realize this was an abnormal reaction, as I had typically refused to accept failure.

I was the oldest child in a family where perfection was expected and displays of emotion were discouraged. Mistakes and emotional outbursts were considered signs of weakness, so I learned to push myself mercilessly and hold everything inside. I sought people who didn't make mistakes. I avoided people who had problems, even avoided funerals, just to deny my emotions. Now I believe that my need to be perfect and my habit of "stuffing" a lifetime of emotions placed an enormous amount of stress on my immune system. These factors did not directly cause my cancer, but they certainly contributed to it.

The Saturday after I received my life-changing news, I encountered the voice of God. His presence began to give me peace in this impossible situation. I would not have said at the time that I heard God's voice, but I believe He spoke through my conscience, saying, "You are not going to die from this. It's a wakeup call."

The next day my husband, uncharacteristically, shared my situation with our Sunday school class. Soon one of our class friends, also a Women's Community Bible Study member, called me. A constant six-month flow of care for me and my family quickly followed. For the first time in my life I was able to allow myself to be loved and nurtured, to feel no guilt for being imperfect, and even to share my emotions. I virtually floated through multiple surgeries and chemotherapy, supported by the love, prayers, and support of God's many messengers.

Afterward, I wanted to help others as I had been helped, so I became a Stephen minister (lay counselor). The monthly meetings I attended immersed me in a completely different atmosphere from my previous life. Everyone was so nurturing. I felt like I was learning to ice skate at age fifty, as I began to learn the skills of nurturing others—and myself.

I joined WCBS, and since then God has continued guiding me along this new path of nurture and care. Each year my small group has led me through the next step in opening myself. In the first year, a group hug would have terrified me. Years later, I have felt confident enough to share my story, my emotions, and lots of hugs. God has provided the love and nurturing; the gift of my cancer has given me permission to accept these blessings, as well as the greater gift of loving and nurturing others.

How incredible You are, O God, that You answer our prayers in ways so much greater than we could ever ask. May we continue to come to You in prayer, trusting You to hear and answer our every need.

Barbara Brown

For God so loved the world . . . John 3:16
He will never leave you nor forsake you. Deuteronomy 31:6
This is my command: Love each other. John 15:17

God's Hand

My life growing up was a troubled one—each year seemed to bring more difficult and complex problems. While my family was educated, morally upright, and loving in many ways, emotional and mental chaos reigned. My parents professed to be believers, but they were never grounded in Christian doctrine and certainly did not attend church. Nevertheless, God seemed to continually call me to Him. I learned about Jesus when I was four or five from my next-door neighbor and will always remember asking my beautiful mother who this "Jesus" was. I don't think she said much, but in her lovely melodic voice she sang "Jesus Loves Me," and I was mesmerized. I had her sing it over and over until I learned each word, so I could sing it myself, which I did almost obsessively. We repeated this process with the Christmas carols "Silent Night," "Away in a Manger," and "O Little Town of Bethlehem." How I loved it when we sang those songs every Christmas. I was too young to understand that God had His hand upon me already.

Several years ago, after the death of my greatest mentor and inspiration, a close friend insisted that I sign up for a Bible study course at Women's Community Bible Study. I was physically and spiritually exhausted, and even though I had asked Christ into my life many years before, I had little desire to participate in a Bible study with a group of "perfect" Christian women. I felt like few people had suffered as much as I had, so what could this group possibly have to offer during this particularly difficult time in my life? My friend was relentless in spite of my resistance and finally appeared at my front door one day with a WCBS application in hand. I was too tired to argue. It was one of the few times in my life that I just submitted, was obedient, and did what I was told to do!

Now, years later, I understand that God, with His hand still upon me, guided me to some of the most inspiring women I have ever known. While they seemed perfect, many of them were also struggling with the memories of difficult childhoods; the complexities of living each day with a chronic illness or addiction; serious family problems; and even the devastating loss of precious spouses, children, or friends. I have been humbled by the way God has so faithfully been present whenever I sought Him—or even when I didn't. I'm finally beginning to understand that when we pray for one another, our most heartfelt prayers are powerful beyond comprehension, and that when God has His hand upon us, He simply does not let go.

Heavenly Father, thank You for Your hand upon my life. Give me strength to reach out to hold the hand of another person who needs You today. Amen.

Marianne Craft

God so loved the world that He gave His only Son, so that everyone who believes in Him will not perish but will have eternal life. John 3:16

My Primary Guide for Living

Everyone has a story. My father was an unemployed alcoholic, and my mother worked hard, making many sacrifices. I grew up with the anxiety of never having quite enough. Eventually I became a Christian, but I didn't know the real joy of the Christian life. I married and had a child, and in 1980 we joined Peachtree Presbyterian Church because it was the "right thing" to do.

While I had always believed in God and accepted that Jesus Christ, His only Son, came to earth, died for the sins of the world, and rose from the grave, I focused on living in the material world. Since I had so little growing up, an empty place of need had developed within me, which I yearned to fill by accumulating material possessions. So the race was on—trying to keep up with the neighbors, attempting to raise the best (smartest, cutest, most athletic) kids, constantly striving to have more and to do better—all so I could fill my empty space within. I ended up in a major health crisis because of my incessant anxiety and inevitable dissatisfaction. I developed severe arthritis and was forced to leave my job because the pain had become so severe. Eventually I had to undergo a total hip replacement, and I was forced to be at home alone! Although this was one of the most difficult periods of my life both physically and emotionally, it was exactly at that time that I was presented with the opportunity to join Women's Community Bible Study. Since I suffered from "good girl syndrome," I rarely missed a study and faithfully completed my homework. God's timing is always perfect, because although I began WCBS with my usual disciplined, "gotta get the job done" approach, God softened my heart as I became more knowledgeable about His works and His Word.

Six years later, I still have my problems, but the Bible has become my primary resource for living. I genuinely understand the meaning of the "peace that passes all understanding" because God has blessed me with the divine gift of faith and the courage to share it. I now realize that the only thing that truly matters is eternal life, and my life has been enriched by this awareness. While one of the greatest blessings I've experienced is the change that has occurred in me through yielding myself to God's design for my life, the ripple effect of blessings is immeasurable. I can finally allow my family to be who God wants them to be without the daily pressure of my unrealistic expectations. Now that I know God controls everything, I can experience the true joy of freedom in myriad ways. In particular, the freedom to serve Him when the Holy Spirit prods has brought significant new relationships into my life that have been incredibly enriching.

My desire to love, serve, and obey Christ took a long time to develop, but I guess God was working with a slow and stubborn learner. It is so comforting to know that throughout the entire process, He patiently and lovingly guided me all the way. Staying in His Word makes me realize just how spectacular heaven is going to be, and I praise and thank God that I believe!

Heavenly Father, thank You for the peace You give me as I trust and believe in You for all things! Amen.

Jo Ditzel

For God has not given us a spirit of fear, but of power and of love and of a sound mind. 2 Timothy 1:7

The Charge of the Christ Brigade

In 2000, a miracle happened in my life. After twenty years of marriage and a diagnosis of infertility, I found out I was going to have a baby. When I shared the news with my wonderful husband, he wasn't struck mute like Zechariah, but he certainly was speechless for a few weeks! We shared our news with family and friends. After they picked their chins up from the ground and their glazed eyes cleared, we all rejoiced.

My pregnancy went fine until the eighth month. Then I developed high blood pressure and was on my way to toxemia. The doctors decided to induce labor as I continued to get sicker. For the next thirty-six hours many things went wrong. The baby and I were both in distress; we lost her heartbeat several times. Due to an allergic reaction to medication and the toxemia, I was also at great risk.

Finally our daughter, Erin, was born, and although she weighed only four pounds, eight ounces, doctors assured us she would be fine. We left the hospital after a week, and for the next two months all was well. I knew Erin was healthy when she reached six pounds. It was then that I fell apart. I stopped sleeping, eating, and developed severe panic disorder. I was put on medication that actually made my condition worse. As my illness grew, I became filled with hopelessness and unbearable depression. Let me tell you, when Satan hears that door of vulnerability creak open, he comes crashing in. Before long I entertained thoughts of suicide. The tempter shows no mercy.

Then the bugles sounded at the Women's Community Bible Study. My dearest friend asked her small group to hold me up in prayer. On hearing of my illness, an incredible woman from the Bible study asked my husband to have me call her. God was starting to assemble an army of Christian women to throw into my path. I called this precious woman (a total stranger), and she talked to me with such warmth and understanding that I was blown away. She told me how God worked in her life and then began to pray with me. This was a totally new experience to me. I didn't even know that prayer "took" over the phone, but an amazing power came through that line.

That very day, my aunt called and said that God was sending her my physical symptoms to let her know of my pain. For the second time, I was being prayed for, courtesy of God and BellSouth. She taught me the Scripture from 2 Timothy and I started praying it constantly.

God kept putting other people from the Bible study in my path, and family and friends poured out their love and support in every way imaginable. However, the medicine continued to make my condition worse, and I hit "rock bottom." The morning I was being sent to an Atlanta hospital, the phone rang and it was the same dear woman who had prayed with me before. Again God had let her know I was in trouble. Talk about supernatural! God has given her the special gift of connecting people in crisis with those who can help. She called yet another member of WCBS who I now call my "earth angel." This awesome woman shared her knowledge of this hospital, of my illness, and also gave generously of her prayers and friendship. She, too, became part of my Christ Brigade.

God has been so faithful and loving. He put me with the right doctors who diagnosed me with post-traumatic stress disorder from delivery complications, and now I have the right treatment. More important, He has shown me the need for Him in my life. He has filled my dark place with the Holy Spirit and given me a voracious appetite for His Word. He has filled me with a joy I have never known that allows me to really appreciate all of His blessings, especially my daughter.

You have probably figured out that now I am a member of WCBS. I thrive on the fellowship I find there every week. Thank You, God, for these awesome women and most of all for your Son, my Savior, Jesus Christ.

Dear Lord, thank You that You go before me in wisdom and grace; that You have given me a spirit of power and love and of a sound mind. Fill me with Your Holy Spirit so that I may conquer my fears and abide with You in peace. Amen.

Betsy Echols

Whom have I in heaven but You? I desire You more than anything on earth. My heart may fail, and my spirit may grow weak, but God remains the strength of my heart; He is mine forever. Psalm 73:26

A Resurrected Dream

My heart was pounding with Richter-scale force. My dreams were coming true! Surrounded by friends and family in an old English-style wedding, my father was walking me down the aisle to marry the beautiful man I had trusted God to bring to me. He had certainly gone above and beyond my imagination. Our marriage had a storybook beginning: "The Alabama football star weds the adoring Old Miss beauty queen."

From the beginning, my husband and I were drawn together in prayer meetings for Campus Crusade for Christ. How I fell in love with his honesty in talking to God. As we grew closer to God, our love grew deeper and stronger. I knew what it meant to be a well-nourished wife who unreservedly honored her husband.

My husband was becoming well-known as a speaker and as a successful Christian attorney. We diligently sought God for wisdom and discernment in influencing others. It was a delight to stand with him, praying for and supporting this man of God. He depended heavily on my input, and we treasured our relationship with God.

Some fifteen years later, we were invited to pastor a parish in Switzerland. Our ministry had a tremendous impact on this community, and seeing the evidence of God at work in their lives prompted my husband to examine his own life. Consequently, when we returned to the States, he announced that he was leaving the law practice and going into full-time ministry. I was shocked. We had always prayed and discussed at length any change before a decision was made. I wish I could say I wholeheartedly supported my husband's decision, but I resisted this dramatic change. I could not handle his shutting me out of his life and putting me so far down in his priorities.

Sensing I was losing my soul mate and torn apart by his no longer seeming to need me, I turned to alcohol. Scared, alone, and rejected, I forgot about God's desire to bless me. On the outside, I projected a facade of "everything is fine," but inwardly I could not bear my husband's disapproval. Leading two lives, I became bitter and resentful because my dreams were being shattered. Years of pain and malcontent took their diabolical toll on us. Yet, even in this horrendous state, there was something inside of me that could not let go of God. I realize now that it was His faithfulness and love carrying me during this dark season.

Eventually my husband and I divorced and I moved back to Atlanta, where my relationship with God flourished. I began attending Women's Community Bible Study. Surrounded by women who desired God's presence, I blossomed. The love, encouragement, and attentiveness I received at WCBS helped bring me from a place of emotional death to a truly fulfilled spiritual life.

We praise You, God, that even when our hearts fail, You are our strength.

Candace Croft Ford

Trust in the LORD with all your heart and lean not on your own understanding. Proverbs 3:5

A New Beginning

I grew up in a devout Roman Catholic family. I attended Mass each Sunday and even served as a lay eucharistic minister. Yet I never really focused on my relationship with Jesus until I experienced a divorce from my husband of twenty-two years. During this period of overwhelming sadness and concern for my three daughters, a friend invited me to her Bible study.

At that time my two oldest daughters had gone to college, and my house was being sold. I did not know where I would be living or what I would be doing. I was afraid of the future. Even worse was the stigma I felt as a Roman Catholic divorcée. Whether I brought it on myself or it was the result of comments of others, I felt embarrassed and humiliated because my marriage had failed. The strength and devotion of the members of the Bible study led me to achieve a strength of conviction that God was in charge. I learned that all I had to do was to turn my life over to Him and trust in Him. We prayed daily that Christ would work in my life to bring me peace. Truly prayers were the golden threads that kept my life together. In retrospect, I see that God took charge and pulled me out of an unhealthy situation and put me in a place where I could grow and flourish, fulfilling God's plans for me.

In addition to trusting that God would take care of me, at this time I developed a personal relationship with Jesus. I had never before read the Scriptures, and doing so humanized my Lord and Savior so that He became my personal friend. I came to feel His presence every day; it was like having a best friend with me always to carry my burdens. In the last decade, I have learned that just as true love for one's spouse and family grows and matures over the years and differs from the infatuation of temporary romance, so true love for Jesus does not vacillate depending on whether one is in trouble and in need of His healing grace. I find that by being with and talking to Jesus every day, His presence in my life becomes stronger and stronger.

I do not believe that there is a necessary correlation between earthly blessings and a close relationship with Jesus. I was blessed, however, in that almost immediately after my divorce I met and fell in love with an extraordinary man. He ended up becoming my husband and with him came two wonderful children. Our two families became one quickly after our marriage, so much so that my "new" daughter (I abhor the term *step*) is the godmother of my oldest daughter's first child.

I pray that my personal relationship with Jesus will continue to grow throughout the rest of my life and that I can truly become an instrument of His peace, striving to do His will in everything I do.

God, I have grown to trust and depend on You for all things; You have blessed me as I've allowed You to direct my paths. Thank You. Amen.

Cynthia Butterfield Glover

The LORD is my shepherd, I shall not be in want. He makes me lie down in green pastures, he leads me beside quiet waters, he restores my soul. He guides me in paths of righteousness for his name's sake. Even though I walk through the valley of the shadow of death, I will fear no evil, for you are with me; your rod and your staff, they comfort me. Psalm 23:1-4

The Lord Is My Shepherd

Life is full of challenges, some good and some bad. The common denominator of challenges is that they make you grow in ways that are hard to anticipate. Your growth may be intellectual, emotional, spiritual, or physical, but it will probably be some combination of these.

Six years ago I was diagnosed with ALS, or Lou Gehrig's disease. ALS is a neurological disease for which there is no known cause or known cure. The neurons that transmit messages from the brain to the body die. Muscles atrophy and in time total paralysis results while the mind remains clear. Life expectancy is two to five years from diagnosis.

I suppose no one is ever prepared for such news. I certainly was not. I was in my prime as a wife, mother, friend, community volunteer, and successful interior designer. I was self-sufficient and in control of my own destiny. How foolish that notion seems in retrospect.

I grew up as a Presbyterian in a small rural community in South Carolina where nearly everyone attended church every Sunday. I was active in the church and served as president of the youth group for several years. My husband and I joined the Episcopal

Church, and I volunteered to teach Sunday school. I considered myself a Christian, but now I know my relationship with God was only a nodding acquaintance; on my list of priorities, my relationship with God probably didn't make the top ten.

Facing my own mortality certainly put a different focus on what was really important. Shortly after my diagnosis I met with the leader of Women's Community Bible Study in the chapel and poured out my heart to God. I shed many tears over the physical, emotional, and financial burden I feared for my family. The thought of my children growing up without their mother seemed unbearable.

She invited me to join WCBS, and what a blessing it has been. I depend on my friends to get me there. Every week I am in the company of Christian women, some who are new in their faith, some who are searching for answers. All of them have the same goal: developing a more intimate relationship with God. I always leave from our time together with new insights and a renewed spirit.

Am I reconciled to this terrible disease? Absolutely not! I fight for my former life every day. But "why me?" was never a question for me. Why not me? Why not you?

I would love to be able to hug my children, hang an ornament on the Christmas tree, or simply walk across the room. But, oh the blessings I've seen. Old friends, new friends, and unknown friends have formed a Christian army to dispense love, compassion, and support. For example, one friend visits every Wednesday and Friday afternoon and helps with personal and family requirements. Another friend delivers my groceries each week. Another friend sends me ALS research information. Yet another friend brings lunch and conversation each Tuesday, and every Monday a small group of WCBS friends conduct Bible study at my home. God has also sent me an especially wonderful Christian woman who gets me through the practical tasks of daily living. She sings His praises all day long!

"The LORD is my shepherd . . . though I walk through the valley of the shadow of death, I will fear no evil, for thou art with me." These words from Psalm 23 really do restore my soul. God and I talk each day. Now I turn everything over to Him—sometimes I take it back, but I am no longer spiritually self-sufficient. He has done so much for me and asks so little in return, simply that I trust Him.

God is good and I am so blessed.

Dear Father, thank You for the comfort that can come only from You as You quiet my heart and restore my soul! Amen.

Tricia Hargett

"For surely I know the plans I have for you," says the Lord, "plans for your welfare and not for harm, to give you a future with hope." Jeremiah 29:11

One of the Sweetest Blessings

There are no words to describe my love for God through Women's Community Bible Study. I joined this Bible study in 1992, when we were still meeting in a small chapel. Many Wednesday mornings, I couldn't wait to get there early just to have time by myself in that incredible room. The smell of the chapel still brings back sweet memories for me. Now as the sanctuary is three-fourths full every Wednesday, I marvel at the lifetime friendships that have blossomed through the years and grow stronger every day.

Never has there been a Wednesday morning that I have gone home sad or defeated. If anything, the homework, the commentaries, the lesson discussion, and prayer time in small groups have given me a great hunger for more of His Word. I am truly amazed at how each lesson seems to hit me on all sides! I am always convicted of something that God is trying to show me, and He never fails to bring up that one thing that I need to hear. This Bible study has given me a greater knowledge of the Bible and a desire to apply what I've learned in my own life and to share it with family and friends. It has helped me become more aware of the needs of others beyond my small world.

A few years ago, I had to give up Wednesday morning Bible study for a while. I think God wanted to grow and stretch me way beyond my comfort zone and allow me to trust only Him! He was teaching me that great lesson of "I can't, but God can."

Sam, my incredible, talented husband, and I were reinventing the Humpty-Dumpty family; we were ready to crumble and fall! We moved from the dream home Sam and I had built together, the home where our children had spent much of their childhood. I did not want to leave my neighbors, close friends, and familiar surroundings. I wanted to hold on to those great memories.

But our heavenly Father had other plans for us and clearly brought us to our knees. In one year my small world began to unravel. We moved from our home, renovated another home while living there, our son left for boarding school in the middle of his eighth-grade year, our daughter was a typical teenager, our marriage was falling apart, Sam's health was at an all-time low (two retinal detachments of each eye within two weeks) *and* I went back to work full-time, teaching first grade. Believe it or not, I experienced incredible strength and joy through many of those trials.

That year while working, I missed my friends. I yearned for the beautiful Wednesday mornings at Bible study and the prayer accountability. I had a strong faith that had been nurtured throughout the years, and I knew without a doubt that God would never forsake me. There was never a day during our brokenness that He didn't provide for me. He filled my cup and gave me what I needed for each day . . . one day at a time. I was asked to teach the chapel services on Friday morning for the children, parents, and teachers at my little school, and I was so excited! The children brought love and joy to me as they entered my first-grade classroom every morning.

That same year, Sam became a believer, and I learned a lot about that little word *submission.* I learned I had to give up trying to do things on my own as well as many other great lessons.

Today, I'm back in Bible study on Wednesday mornings, and my family has never been stronger. Sam and I will soon celebrate twenty-five years of marriage. We are centered in Christ's love, and our Humpty-Dumpty family has been put back together beautifully! And not by the king's men but by the King Himself! Sam is the spiritual leader in our home, we are whole, together, and our children are living examples of God's grace.

God has used the Bible study to give me godly friendships that will last forever, boundless laughter, the thrill of doing skits, and a joy and desire to continue to build my relationship with Jesus Christ. I will forever cherish the love and warmth that pour out of these walls every week when I enter this holy place. WCBS is one of the sweetest blessings in my life, and I will always be thankful that this group has become not only a passion but also a second family.

Wise and loving God, help us always to trust in Your plans for us.

Cindy Hewlett

I will thank you Lord, in front of all the people. I will sing praises among the nations. Psalm 108:3

Praising God

I am a vessel of God. Through my times of hurt and sorrow, He has filled me with peace, compassion, and the strength to endure. I am indebted to Him: "In my distress I prayed to the Lord, and the Lord answered me and rescued me" (Psalm 118:5). As I submit to God, I am willing to give back all that I possibly can in gratitude for all God had given me.

My life has been quilted with an array of circumstances: I have lived in an unhappy marriage; felt the pain, anguish, and loss of divorce with my children; and by the grace of God, with few financial resources, I have managed to live and provide for them, all the while trusting in God's providence. In return, God has truly provided for me. I have been blessed with a wonderful husband and a comfortable life for me and for my children. I am so grateful for the blessings that are more than I can count!

Wanting to express my gratitude through a deeper faith, I joined Women's Community Bible Study. I felt I had so much to share with others, and doing so would allow me to return thanks to God. As it turned out, things have happened differently than I thought that they would. In my eight years with WCBS, my giving back has developed more slowly, and I have received so much more. The maturity I thought I had was far from developed. While trying to survive my own difficulties, I missed learning about other women's lives; therefore, I had a lot of catching up to do. God has really worked with me in this fertile environment through the sharing and community of the women in this study. As a result, I have grown mightily in its safe and loving fellowship. There is something very special about a committed body of Christ and the way in which it is guided. I have experienced God's presence among us each week. We are all committed to live more fully the Christian life of faith. "Give thanks to the Lord, for He is good, His faithfulness endures forever" (Psalm 118:1).

Father, thank You that in my darkest hour, You strengthened me and gently led me to a group of women with whom I could share this journey of life and faith. Thanks be to God!

Susan E. Kyle

*God made you alive with Christ. He forgave us all our sins, having
canceled the written code, with its regulations, that was against us. . . .
He took it away, nailing it to the cross. Colossians 2:13,14*

*Transformed
by the Cross*

I grew up in North Carolina in a family where there was great
tragedy and pain. I learned that strength is not found in how in-
tensely one struggles, but in how intently one surrenders to God.
The need for love and acceptance filled my life with isolation and
heartache. I knew God was real, but I would not make a commitment to follow Him, even though I was lonely and hurting.

Although God began to seek me early in my life, offering me
unconditional love, approval, and acceptance, I wasn't willing to
give my life to Him. Throughout my life I have struggled with
addictions, paralyzing wise decision making.

I married a wonderful man and we joined the Peachtree Presbyterian Church. We soon became immersed in the life of the
church. Because addiction was a large component of my life, money,
power, and politics became my drugs of choice.

I was tapped to enter politics and was elected first vice chair of
the Republican Party for the Fifth Congressional District in Atlanta. I attended events, dinners, and cocktail affairs in Washing-
ton and was involved in policy meetings, serving on important
committees, and making speeches.

Through a series of bad choices and my lack of maturity, I
found myself involved in a federal sting operation and was charged
and jailed with seven felony counts of money laundering.

The private and public hell I began to endure opened the door to God. I learned that salvation only comes from a cross.

I humbly received God's gift of forgiveness and committed my life to Him. I learned that "He gives strength to the weary and increases the power of the weak." God began the gentle process of healing and reshaping my life.

In retrospect, the pain and shame became the best thing that has ever happened to me. God carried me through the humiliation of being featured on the front pages of the paper—not in a ball gown but behind a face of shame and humiliation.

God carried me through the long days of court and took me to my family to ask for the money for my legal defense.

God spoke directly to me and said, "I love you, I've willingly paid the penalty you owed, and I have forgiven you. But there are penalties for forgiven sin. Trust Me and follow Me."

I followed Him into a federal prison and waved good-bye to my husband and our nine-month-old daughter. I learned first-hand about the pain, the isolation, and the heartache of prison; and God was my constant companion.

God uses consequences, suffering, shame, and the accompanying pain to build us up and teach us how to depend on Him. None of it was easy, but He became my best friend, my holy Comforter, and the one that I claim as the core and center of who I am today.

God doesn't promise to take away the pain and suffering of our lives, but He does come into the ravine with us and weathers the storm, anointing us with His wonderful Spirit.

Thank You, Father, for remaking me, refining me by the fire, and assuring me of Your love.

Toni Lansing

And we know in all things God works for the good of those who love Him, who have been called according to His purpose. Romans 8:28

Hope in Adversity

I want to share my testimony because I believe it will give hope to others who face adversity in their lives. When I was five years old, my parents divorced. My alcoholic dad later died of cancer. My mother struggled as a single, working mom. In college, I suffered from an eating disorder. I married an alcoholic while I trying to finish medical school. That marriage ended in divorce. I later remarried during my residency training. My first pregnancy ended in a miscarriage literally during the middle of my medical boards. To state it simply, life as I knew it had not been easy. The easy route, unfortunately, is not how we learn and grow in faith.

As a young girl, I adored my grandmother, whose strong faith stirred my desire to know Christ. On Easter Sunday in 1990, I was "born again." The sermon that day was a compilation of the teachings of C.S. Lewis and Josh McDowell. The premise was that if we believe in Christ, then we must come to terms with who He is. Either He is a liar or a lunatic, or He is the Incarnate Son of God and my Savior. I had never thought of the huge ramifications of this simple concept. I accepted Christ as my Savior during that sermon that day. That was the turning point in my Christian faith.

Several years later, I retired to be at home with my family. I began attending the Women's Community Bible Study, which has helped me grow in my knowledge and faith. It provided a supportive community of Christian women as friends. Only God knew how much I would need them and His truth in the days to follow. I was saved; I knew Jesus; I thought my problems were behind me and only happiness and joy lay ahead. I could not have been more wrong! I was to find that you cannot truly experience the peace and joy of God at the top of the mountain without feeling its distance from the deep and darkest valley.

I think God gets our attention where we are the most vulnerable. For men, the issues seem to be wealth and power; for women, the issues seem to be vanity and our children. In any event, it was through my children that God allowed me to test my faith. Through my daughter's severe eating disorder, I met evil face-to-face. At times, it seemed to possess her. We almost lost her as the disorder began to take over her entire psyche. Only God could intervene in the form of choices for her care, in the prayers of friends, and in the testing of my faith. By God's beautiful grace she is now in recovery. As her faith deepened, she began to sense that she is His child. She realized that the tremendous power of the Holy Spirit was available to her in her struggle with this insidious disease, and each of us was changed.

Facing the challenges this disease exacts on every member of our family has been difficult. It has allowed me to see that though God will never give us more than we can handle, the world is ready and waiting to dish out many challenges. Charles Swindoll says, "Life is 10 percent what happens to you and 90 percent how you respond to it." I have been able to understand God's direction for me by how I respond to situations He permits in my life. These personal issues have called me to demonstrate my faith by helping others who find themselves in similar circumstances. I believe that we respond to God by attempting to make a difference for others. Reflecting God's love is the purpose of life.

Through my children's struggles with learning disabilities and my mother's battle with Alzheimer's disease, I find comfort in knowing that I will never face adversity alone. Christ will never leave me or forsake me. I pray every day to find peace in God's presence, joy in His love, and hope in His promise. I conclude with a prayer I offered at WCBS on January 27, 1999, the day before my daughter concluded her four-month treatment program and came home.

Dear God, help us to realize that each new day is a new beginning for all of us. It is an opportunity to make amends for a hurt, to forgive a wrong, to resolve a conflict, to give love unconditionally, to listen without judging, to extend an act of kindness without expectation, to see the beauty and miracle of life around us, and to realize that what really matters in life are relationships—with our families, with our friends, and with our Savior. Thanks be to God!

Rhonda Milner

The law of the LORD is perfect, reviving the soul. The statutes of the LORD are trustworthy, making wise the simple. The precepts of the LORD are right, giving joy to the heart. Psalm 19:7-8

Faith in All Things Big and Small

I have been fortunate in marriage; this year we celebrate twenty-two years, and we are blessed with a wonderful family and three children. We have been fortunate that my husband's career allowed us to live in my hometown for nearly ten years. Unfortunately, the day came when I had to leave behind my roots.

We have just moved to Atlanta from Houston, leaving cousins, wonderful friends, and our oldest daughter, who is finishing her senior year living with another family. Our move involved lots of logistics: sales of property, visiting colleges with our oldest daughter, and applying to schools with two teenagers who would move with us. I came knowing I had only one childhood friend in Atlanta.

As I did in our move eleven years ago to Houston, my first step was to build a foundation within a church and to become part of a Bible study. These connections and attention to God's Word through regular study and fellowship keep my faith strong and our family grounded. God has been faithful in bringing strong networks to us to pave our way and help us settle. We continue to be blessed.

On many occasions before our move, friends bombarded me with questions: "Where is Kasey going to live?" "Where will your children be in school?" "Have you sold your ranch?" "How are you managing with your husband gone?" (My husband moved seven months ahead of me, leaving me with the details of closing out our lives in Houston and getting us settled in Atlanta.) My friends seemed more stressed than I was, and I felt I needed to remind them that God is faithful, even in the little things.

Repeatedly in prayer I gave the big things over to God to control, and because there were so many details in the move, I even had to surrender to Him in the smallest of things—a true leap of faith! And each step of the way God was there, and His way, although many times not the answer I thought would work, was the right thing, and blessings abounded even in the smallest of details.

Facing the unknown requires leaps of faith, but when you have a joyful heart, trust in the ways of the Lord, and remain faithful in prayer, life can be simple even when it seems overwhelmingly complicated.

Father, You are dependable and perfect in all things. I put my trust in You, and You fill my heart with joy in return. Thank You!

Ann Morton

"For I know the plans I have for you," declares the Lord, "plans to prosper you and not to harm you, plans to give you hope and a future." Jeremiah 29:11

The Secret

Abuse and divorce are ugly words. For most of my life I found it easier to keep "the secret" and to hide the ugliness. Shame and embarrassment can be paralyzing and can overpower good judgment. I learned through experience, though, that sharing the truth can be cathartic and, more importantly, helpful to others. I hope you will find comfort and will be convinced "you are never alone."

My parents were diligent in their Christian teachings, in their example, and in their profession of faith. Divorce was not in our family vocabulary. Marrying my college sweetheart seemed like the right thing to do—until he left me seven years later.

After five years, I married again. This time I was sure it would last. He had accepted Jesus Christ and had been baptized. Our relationship was pure and clean, and the plans we made for our family were much like the ones I had experienced with my own family. However, I found myself in the midst of physical abuse. I blamed myself and was full of shame. It was my secret. Seven years later, he left. In the meantime, I had given birth to a baby boy; a close family member had been admitted to a treatment center for drugs and alcohol; my best friend had died in an airplane crash; and I had been diagnosed with cancer. I threw up my hands in desperation and confusion.

The three H's, hapless, helpless, and hopeless, became my best friends. I had given up on help; I had given up on me; and I had given up on God. It was a dry, lonely place. Ironically, I remember praying for the strength to go forward and praying for God to be with me as I sorted out the questions.

Today, God continues to bless me beyond my imagination. I have a wonderful Christian husband who has been like a real father to my son. For fifteen years God has shown me wonderful things about me, about His love for me, and about forgiveness.

So much in life is "about me," about how I respond to the world around me. God has given me enumerable opportunities to be with others in their pain, blame, and shame and has helped me redefine pride, ego, and judgment. I know of no other place like the Women's Community Bible Study where so many have the opportunity to refine and perfect their faith.

Deliberately I had search for the Bible study that would fulfill my deepest desires to know God intimately. Six years ago I joined WCBS, where opportunities to expand and improve as a Christian woman are immeasurable and where special talents are developed and refined through writing, leading, training, organizing, speaking and facilitating. Christian peers have provided the support and love needed for me to be able to carefully scrutinize my responses to the world around me, culminating in the intimacy with Jesus Christ for whom I had longed.

Faithful Father, I praise your Holy name for always being with me. I thank you with all my heart for the plans You have for me...plans I can hardly wait to experience. Amen.

Anonymous

Come to me, all you who are weary and burdened,
and I will give you rest. Matthew 11:28

The Healing
of a Marriage

I am writing to share the miracle of how Jesus saved my marriage and my family. I grew up in a loving home with a close family. We always said prayers at bedtime and attended church, although I really never got the message.

Later, I was fortunate enough to have a successful modeling career, but all my priorities were wrong. They were all about me. Jesus was not in my life. My career, my body, and my addictions were my idols. I always wanted more and never was content. After ten years of marriage, my husband and I drifted apart, and ultimately both of us were unfaithful. We were headed for divorce. The papers were drawn. We were miserable and guilt-ridden, especially considering our two beautiful baby daughters.

During this terrible time in my life, I cried to God one night, saying, "Please help me!" I expressed sorrow for the things I had done. I told God I just wanted to be a child again so that I would not do the deeds that had led to the destruction in my life. I wasn't sure God heard me, but I was scared enough to try anything. I woke up the next morning with an awesome sense of security and peace that I had never felt before.

I called my best friend and told her something had happened to me. Years before, she had given me a Bible that was gathering dust in a drawer. I hadn't touched it until that moment. When I began reading it, God led me to Matthew 11:28-29: "Come to me, all you who are weary and burdened, and I will give you rest. Take my yoke upon you and learn from me, for I am gentle and humble in heart and you will find rest for your souls."

I felt the biggest load lifted from me, and I yearned to know more about God. I started going to church. I read Scriptures to my (soon to be, I thought, ex-) husband and talked about God with great joy. I am sure he thought I had lost my mind, but over time he saw a different wife—a happy, secure, and peaceful person who begged him to return.

Later he came to church with me and accepted Christ as his Savior! Our attorneys were shocked. They said they had never seen such a damaged marriage come back together. It truly was a miracle!

My husband and I realized that the way to trust each other again was to trust Jesus first. Today I am able to testify that because of Jesus, we have an awesome marriage. I truly love my husband more today than ever because Jesus is the center of our lives. He taught us the importance of *relationship instead of religion,* which has resulted in our experiencing God in a real and personal way. When you ask God to guide you through all you do, you will be amazed at the wonderful turns your life will take.

Lord, You promise to give us rest when our burdens are too heavy to carry ourselves. I pray today for that rest. Amen.

Jenny Pritchett

Come to me, all you who are weary and burdened,
and I will give you rest.
Take my yoke upon you and learn from me,
for I am gentle and humble in heart,
And you will find rest for your souls.
For my yoke is easy and my burden is light.
Matthew 11:28-30

The Beauty of Tears

I cry when I pray out loud. I cry when I hold my prayer partner's hand. I cry when I hear the beautiful songs and music every Wednesday morning at our Women's Community Bible Study. I cry when I hear the inspiring commentaries and testimonies each week. I cry when I look up at the beautiful and peaceful stained-glass window in the sanctuary—and I'm crying right now as I write this testimony. While it may seem that all of my tears could be tears of sorrow, they are not. I have come to understand that both good emotions and divine happiness can create tears of true joy, which represent the profound way in which God is working in my life.

There have been times in my life, especially following the deaths of my parents and a failed marriage, when I felt unworthy of God's love, and these events did result in tears of deep grief and sorrow. It took years of therapy, studying the Word of God, and listening to the tender words of my Bible study leaders to understand that God truly loves me just as I am. My blessed children, their father, and his wife (my children's other mom, whom I dearly love) have been mighty illustrations of God's presence in my life, for they love me just as much as I love them. Our unique situation tells me that I am God's special child, that He loves me unconditionally, and that our blended family, which could have been permanently damaged by the effects of a broken marriage, has actually been made whole in our love for one another and God's abiding love for each one of us. My greatest prayer is that I will continue to grow in my faith and be able to walk with my heavenly Father holding my hand all the way.

Father God, thank You for tears of joy that remind me of the rest I have found in You. Amen.

Ann Richards

"For I know the plan I have for you," declares the LORD, "plans to prosper you and not to harm you, plans to give you hope and a future. Then you will call upon me and come and pray to me and I will listen to you. You will seek me and find me when you seek me with all your heart." Jeremiah 29:11-13

The Unexpected Plan

It is no easy task to put your life on paper. As the words describing my deepest, most sacred moments take shape, they seem to dance around the page with a private insight all their own. Yet it is gracefully empowering to trace God's hand in every word and phrase illustrating the crucial markers of my life. As I recount the narrative God intended, I begin to understand how my life fits into the larger story—the story that begins and ends with Him.

I was born the third daughter of parents deeply rooted in the South and firmly entrenched in the Baptist tradition. They were strong in faith, discipline, and Christian values; as a result, my childhood was filled with a secure love and pervasive sense of God's immanence. My adolescent and young adult years did not change my world view; my life mirrored the idyllic lives of many American youths with advantage and security. The last decade of my life, however, produced three defining events that reshaped my faith and led me with a deeper passion into the loving arms of God.

For most, marriage is a catalyst for change, and mine was no exception. But when God surprised me with a Jewish partner, I was compelled to sharpen the blurred edges of my beliefs and the true depth of my commitment to Christ. Marriage was a passage that shaped and clarified the direction for my life, and it gave me a certainty of my convictions. As God wove my husband and me together in heritage and faith, He drew us nearer to Him. Today, as I count my blessings, I count my husband twice.

A few years later, the birth of our daughter filled my days with a fresh sense of divine presence, and with it an urgency to deepen my faith. This pull toward the sacred placed God front-and-center in my life; I fell in love with Him all over again. My heart soars every time I look into my daughter's face and encounter the beauty and mystery of God's immense gift.

During the bliss of our daughter's first year, I would name her baptism as the most powerful moment of my life. Yet I would soon realize that God's transforming power can blanket us both in joy and in sorrow. Just a few months later, my twenty-five-year-old brother was diagnosed with cancer. Having just graduated from Emory University and at a seminal point in his career and in his life, he was stricken fiercely with the disease. After ten crucial months of caring for my brother, covering him in fervent prayer, and "bargaining" with God, I lost him. Time stood still for me. His death was an event so excruciatingly painful, and yet extraordinarily transforming; it was my "dark night of the soul," described by the Spanish poet and monk St. John of the Cross. My soul ached, but God's presence was constant and palpable, and I still marvel at His immense power of healing.

God honors us with His promises in the very depth of our pain. Embracing me with His strength, God gently took my hand and led me to a women's Bible study that became, literally, the arms of His love. I found that in seeking a deeper relationship with Christ, Bible study and prayer are the passionate means toward aligning my heart with His. Each week, as we enter the sanctuary to study God's word, we walk over the threshold from the secular to the sacred and become equals in the body of Christ.

Women's Community Bible Study is home, a place of peace and joy and transformation. I am awed by the magnitude of faith and worship within this Bible study, and I am humbled by God's presence, fully in our midst, touching each of us with His plans of grace, hope, and abiding love.

Abba, Father, I place my hand in Yours and look forward with great anticipation to the future You have prepared for me. Keep me on my knees before You, Lord, calling upon Your holy name and seeking You with all my heart. It is in your Son's name, my Lord and Savior, Jesus Christ, that I live and pray. Amen.

Sheila Shessel

In God, whose word I praise, in God I trust; I will not be afraid. What can mortal man do to me? All day long they twist my words; they are always plotting to harm me. Psalm 56:4-5

A Mother's Despair, A Mother's Hope

The process of turning my life over to my heavenly Father began with a tumultuous marriage and divorce, which resulted in a broken home for my two precious daughters. For years, I had been so self-centered and filled with pride that I found it difficult to be accountable for my own actions, and I was quick to blame others for the mess my life had become. Little did I realize during this phase of my life that God already had a wonderful plan to draw me close to Him, which entailed using my musical abilities for *His* glorification. I was trained as a pianist, but I was definitely not trained to play for religious organizations or to accompany singers of God-inspired music. So, as my life fell apart before my very eyes, God was setting the stage to resurrect my precious little family—all through music!

While my daughters and I were still in deep grief and transition following my divorce, I was introduced to Women's Community Bible Study. At that time, WCBS was just a small group of women who were committed to studying God's Word every week, beginning in the fall and ending in late spring. Every Wednesday morning, we met in a tiny chapel of a large church to hear a commentary on the lesson we had studied the previous week. We then broke into small groups for a more intimate life application study and, as just as important, for fellowship. However, worship music of any type was not a part of our Wednesday mornings. As emotionally exhausted as I was, I felt called to volunteer to play the piano—to play both hymns and other types of traditional church music—before the commentary each week. This was just the beginning of how God was calling me to realize His faithful presence in my life, but at the time, I don't think I had a clue as to exactly who was doing the calling! Amazed as I was to be playing the piano for a small Bible study, God had even greater plans to reveal His loving presence to me.

God brought a beautiful woman with an exquisite voice to my home one afternoon in early spring. We were to rehearse for the end-of-the-year Bible study program, but I had never met her. As I tentatively began to play the pieces that had been selected for the program and she began to sing, I dissolved into tears. My heart was so deeply touched by the anointing of God through her beautiful voice that I began to weep deep tears of grief and remorse. My new friend—my angel—sat down next to me on the piano bench, tenderly put her arm around me, and gently asked if she could lift me up in prayer. That was the real beginning of my spiritual journey.

For the first time in my life, I began to let go—and the evolving process of finally allowing Jesus to be my continual source of strength and comfort began. As I was confronted with making critical decisions for my little family as a single parent, I learned to fall to my knees and cry out, "Help me, Lord!" Often the pain was unbearable, but I learned to pray—and wait to hear His voice. With each situation that arose, the power of answered prayer became more profoundly evident to me. I was awed to realize that I was truly becoming a believer! Inevitably, God's angels always appeared in my moments of greatest need to offer hope and encouragement.

Now, each day is becoming an accumulation of miracles—from the way God has used my musical abilities for His purpose to the way He is faithfully present in my family as we continue to heal. I praise Him mightily for drawing me closer and closer, not only through music but in all of the challenges of my daily life.

Heavenly Father, I will forever be grateful because I know that I am in the comforting arms of Jesus Christ, my Savior and my Lord. Amen.

Mary Jane Theden

The Lord is my shepherd: I shall not want. He maketh me to lie down in green pastures. He restoreth my soul. Psalm 23:1-3

Always There

One thing I realize as I look back over my life is that God has never left me. He has *always* been there for me, even though I have wandered away from Him on numerous occasions.

As I reflect back, I realize how blessed I was to be raised in a Christian home. I learned the Ten Commandments, the Beatitudes, the Lord's Prayer, and various Bible verses not only in Sunday school, but through elementary school teachers as well. In times of great distress, these verses have sustained me over the years. Yet, like any teenager, I could not wait to get to college so that I could set my own agenda. Eventually my agenda took me away from God, but God did not leave me. For more than fifteen years I was on this journey—for you see, Satan is as subtle in his endeavor to draw us away from our beliefs as God is to guide us through this life. Finally, after I nearly wrecked my whole life, I realized that I needed to go back to my basic Christian roots and start all over again. God just kept hanging on to me—He kept pulling me back to Him, until I had no one but God and my parents. Through prayer and love from family and friends, I began to see the light. Early in my life I had memorized the Twenty-third Psalm, and when all else seemed to disappear from my memory, I was able to hang on to that beautiful psalm.

The breakup of my first marriage started me on my renewal journey with God, and that journey has only grown with each passing year. Learning and realizing that I needed to do some forgiving, including forgiving myself, was a total shock. God spoke to me through my present husband, Hugh, regarding forgiveness.

Hugh and I had many conversations and searched out many Bible verses on forgiveness. Eventually I was able to make the phone call and say, "I forgive you; I hope you can forgive me." I cannot put into words what freedom that statement gave me. I still marvel today when I think about the release it brings to my heart. How different my life has been because I finally got the message and made the phone call. It was the beginning of the end, the beginning of not looking back, but of looking forward, to a new life. The next part of the journey was to forgive myself. That has taken much longer and I'm still working on it, but I have learned so much in that part of my journey that the yesterday of my life no longer overshadows the present. God is the focus now!

These past twenty-plus years since I took that fork in the road have taken me down new paths in my walk with God—to enlightening Bible studies, to travel all over the world, and through a roller-coaster ride of experiences with my children and stepchildren. I am thankful every day that God has been with me. What I realize the most as I reflect back is how blessed I have been and how God has *never* given up on me. He has guided me every step of the way. When the moments of guilt, doubt, and frustration come, I know that God *is* near and that I, a forgiven sinner, can turn to Him because Christ died for my sins. Hallelujah!

Dear Shepherd, I pray not only for the restoration of my soul but all the other wandering souls in this world.

Claudia Walker

*In you my soul takes refuge. I will take refuge
in the shadow of your wings. Psalm 57:1*

An Unusual Faith Journey

My faith was as unusual as the blue and gold cross I wore on a chain around my neck when I began my faith journey with Women's Community Bible Study. The vertical part of my cross was an aquamarine crystal that would help me cover all the bases if my New Age beliefs won over my traditional Christian upbringing. At the time, Buddhism and Judaism looked interesting to me; however, I also wanted to investigate Christianity more deeply. As my first year of Bible study progressed, I took a leap of faith and decided to commit to Christ, but I went about life as usual, unsuspecting that my life would soon drastically change. One stifling summer day after my first year in Bible study, my husband took his life. Stephen was a doctor who provided our family with many material possessions. We had a big house in town, a house in the mountains, children in the right private school, and fancy cars. Yet, like Stephen, I felt insecure and longed for meaning. I had spent most of my time trying to achieve the picture-perfect life. Obviously, after Stephen's death, appearing perfect was impossible.

Thank God for my Bible study that emotionally supported me after Stephen's death. Six lawyers had to sort out our estate, and when they finished delving into our finances, they informed me that our empire was built on sand. There wasn't much money left for the children and me, and I was so devastated that all I could do was turn to God. Church, Bible study, and my Christian friends were my support, and I felt God's protection and love while I built a relationship with Him. Yet, I still felt sorry for myself because of all the possessions I'd lost. Then God did an amazing thing for me. When the missions committee at First Presbyterian Church needed a few people to visit the tiny village of Muandi on the banks of the Zambezi River to investigate future mission work, God sent my children and me to Africa for five weeks.

The trip to Africa changed my life. This beautiful yet incredibly poor country and its people healed my soul. While working in Muandi's hospital, I met African people with incredible faith. The villagers owned absolutely nothing but mud huts and the clothes on their backs. Daily they depended on the Lord to provide food. I discovered, to my surprise, that the African people were happy and fulfilled, and as I spent time with these kind and gentle people, I noticed how they were able to place everything in God's hands. They enthusiastically rejoiced when something good happened, and they gave thanks to God. They were sad when a loved one died, yet they were sure of an everlasting life. The villagers spent most of their days connected to God, each other, and to the earth. In comparison to the people I knew back home in Atlanta, these Africans seemed happier.

The humble, grateful villagers helped me switch my focus away from myself and toward God and all His blessings. When my focus shifted, I was able to gratefully see God's presence everywhere. Milton described how gratitude can change life by saying, "Gratitude bestows reverence, allowing us to encounter everyday epiphanies, those transcendent moments of awe that change forever how we experience life and the world." Gratitude helped me stop feeling sorry for myself and helped me start living.

Now, back in Atlanta, I try to hold on to the gratitude I feel for having Jesus in my life by remembering that I deserve nothing, yet He has given me everything. I try to leave matters in His hands and not worry about the future. I enjoy the feel of my 100 percent cotton sheets from K-mart as I slip into bed at the end of a busy day of teaching school and thank God for the roof over my head and the food on my table. Often, I think back on my weeks in Muandi and marvel about how God sent me halfway around the world to Africa to save me. I touch my unusual cross as I drift off to sleep and remember how far God has carried me.

Heavenly Father, nothing can separate me from Your love. The fears of today and the worries of tomorrow fall away in the midst of Your glory and grace. I delight in Your presence and abide in Your peace, for my soul takes refuge in the shadow of your wings. Amen.

Kay Whipple

FIVE

When God Changes You . . .

You Become Part of His Family

Rejoice with those who rejoice;
Mourn with those who mourn.   Romans 12:15

We are already into the second or third generation of
people in our culture who have grown up without a sense
of family. The days of "Father Knows Best," "Ozzie and
Harriet," "Leave It to Beaver," and "The Donna Reed Show"
are just distant memories of a better day. Not a perfect
day, but a better one as far as family is concerned.

Many young and middle-aged adults were raised in
nontraditional homes: Single parents, blended families,
extended families, children raising siblings, grandparents
raising grandchildren. The breakdown of the biblical family model has sent shock waves through society. Genera-
tions of people are entering society without the experience of family, a place where identity, honesty, acceptance,
forgiveness, encouragement, instruction, and love
abound. Thankfully, those values are sometimes discov-

ered in other settings—but sometimes they are not.

There is no mistaking the family terminology that is applied to the body of Christ. God is Father, Jesus is pictured as a husband, the church is called the bride of Christ, and Christians are seen as the sons and daughters of God. The church is meant to be the ultimate family experience for its members. Those who pursue a life of obedience to Scripture find themselves drawn more and more deeply into a family; women are drawn into a sisterhood of believers. Accountability, sharing, oneness, openness, friendship, security—everything that a family should be—is experienced as women grow closer to one another in Christ. Many who experienced the warmth and closeness of a human family make an easy transition into the family of God. And those who grew up without a supportive family structure suddenly find a need met that they knew they had but didn't know how to describe. Learning to love, and be loved by, fellow believers in Christ is the ultimate family experience. Many women in this book discovered this family through Women's Community Bible Study.

Regardless of your family background, you'll identify with the experiences of the women who tell their stories in this section. Let them encourage you to enjoy the blessings and benefits of becoming a part of the family of God—both now and for eternity.

So then you are no longer strangers and aliens, but you are fellow citizens with God's people, and are members of God's household. Ephesians 2:19

The Joy
of Community

When I first heard of Women's Community Bible Study, the name told me several things about the group. WCBS seemed to mean that women of the community, perhaps of all denominations, studied the Bible together. I was immediately interested and excited about joining.

After participating in this Bible study for several years, now the name Women's Community Bible Study has a much deeper meaning. It is not only *women of the community* studying the Bible together; it is *a community of women* studying the Bible together. Community, fellowship, friendship, accountability, forgiveness, love, and acceptance—these are glorious aspects of this community of women God has brought together.

This community within the body of Christ welcomes, encourages, and nurtures women from all stations in life, from varied backgrounds, and at different places in our walks with the Lord. We pray with and for each other, and our bond in Christ enables us to share our deepest hopes, joys, and burdens as we learn more about the Lord. God is using this Bible study as an enormous blessing in my life, and I am so thankful to be part of this community.

Heavenly Father, thank You for the privilege of being members of Your household and for bringing communities of women together to worship and serve You.

Elizabeth W. G. Ausband

The LORD's lovingkindnessess indeed never cease, For His compassions
never fail. They are new every morning; Great is thy faithfulness.
Lamentations 3:22-23 NASB

A Love Story

When asked how Christ has made a difference in my life, I began to trace His hand from that particular moment when I gave my life to Him. I surrendered my childhood wounds, the situations I could not fix or control, and on bended knee said to Him, "Lord, I need a Savior; thank You for forgiving me and loving me . . . I am Yours."

When Christ made His home in my heart, my life was never the same. My journey with him reads like a love story with some knocks along the way as His strong-willed child learned what it meant to truly surrender to Him. I knew that I longed to know Him, I longed to please Him, and I deeply desired to be used by Him. And as I look back, I am amazed at how He was always pursuing me, always drawing me to Him through people, experiences, and a restlessness in my heart.

He led me to study His word with gifted teachers. He blessed my husband and me with a challenging Sunday school class, a group of new friends in Christ who were eager to learn and grow. I was also very blessed with a small prayer group who prayed with me and for me, encouraging one another, holding one other accountable, and loving one another for over twenty-five years as we continue to be close, faithful sisters in Christ. I had countless opportunities to serve and to grow in my faith; He always blessed me beyond my wildest dreams. Along the way, I needed to purge some wounds of my past, and with Christ and a few close friends who extended grace to me, I began to heal and break free. I learned to trust in my Lord's flawless character and to walk in the assurance of His love.

It's a process, I stumble and fall often, but I have found that His tender mercies are new each day. Walking in His grace is something I've had to learn over time; it doesn't come easy for someone who is so hard on herself. He began to teach me through His Word who I truly am in Him.

When you realize the reality of a loving Father actively pursuing a love relationship with you in spite of all your weaknesses, the result is a heart full of gratitude and joy. His gift of grace has made all the difference, yet, He once again showered me with another blessing: the gift of His blessed community.

I don't believe anyone was ever aware that when Jesus Christ said, "Follow Me," there would be such a reward in the gathering of seekers and followers. Twelve years ago, Christ nudged me to join thirteen women in a two-year study of the Bible. After much prayer our group was led to help our leader start Women's Community Bible Study. Yes, we were willing and available, but we were also inadequate, a little frightened, and somewhat nervous about surrendering our busy lives to make this commitment. We accepted our Lord's invitation to be involved with Him in His work, and the results were and continue to be amazing. God led me to a place of Christian fellowship and I began to understand the blessings of being in the body of Christ. Every Wednesday for ten years, hundreds of women have gathered to study God's Word and to worship Him. Each one of us is unique in her journey, in her victories, in her Gethsemanes, and in her gifts. Yet we are united in His love as His Holy presence enfolds us there. I have had the joy of witnessing God's power, transforming love, and intimate presence in the lives of so many women. Their faith has inspired and strengthened me, challenged me, and held me accountable to a standard of living that would honor my Lord.

My journey with Christ is a love story indeed, and the best part is knowing the ending will be filled with joyful surprises and everlasting peace.

Thank You, Lord Jesus, for Your grace and for allowing me to experience the fullness of Your grace in this blessed community of holy fellowship. My heart is full of gratitude for Your loving presence in my life always and forever.

Pam Elting

Without faith it is impossible to please God, because anyone who comes to Him must believe that He exists and that He rewards those who earnestly seek Him. Hebrews 11:6

The Rewards of Earnestly Seeking Jesus

Somehow, from an early age I believed in Jesus. Was that because of my mother, who exemplified Jesus' love? Was it the security of having a father who was committed to his church and lived a morally upright life? Was it the Sunday school teachers who taught the stories of Jesus' life? Was it the beautiful church my family attended, where the sun streamed through the stained glass, bringing ecstasy to a young child's heart before that child knew what ecstasy was? I am sure all of these things and more surrounded and convicted me from an early age that Jesus, the Son of God, existed.

I was very blessed to attend a Christian camp that was dedicated to instilling in its campers a hunger for the love of Christ. In high school and college many of the dangerous pathways that my fellow students took did not tempt me because I knew that when God gave us commands, He (in His almighty wisdom) had our good interests at heart. When I chose a husband, I made sure that he understood Christianity and that he understood that I believed that Jesus had lived. I knew that I was richly blessed, but my heart hungered . . . for what?

When children came to our church, I saw to it that they were baptized, confirmed, and that they attended regularly. I was active in church affairs, trying to show my faith that Jesus had lived. But oh, how my heart hungered . . . for what?

A dear friend suggested that I join her at a Bible study. Studying the Bible was a novel idea to me. I could see reasons for studying theology, church history, and the influence of Christianity on civilization. But study the Bible? Whatever for? I knew the stories; I actually believed they were true. I accepted with total faith that Jesus, the Son of God, had lived on earth. Yet, my heart hungered . . . for what?

Bible study was a new experience to me. Studying the actual words of Jesus in the context they were written. Tracing the fulfillment of the prophecies. The intellectual stimulation of earnestly trying to understand how God had communicated with His people. Yet, my heart still hungered . . . for what?

As I became more familiar with the Bible and not just with its stories, I was overwhelmed with the joy of studying the Word. Then one day in one of the small groups, someone asked, "What has Jesus Christ done, and what is He doing in your life?"

As if a great wind had lifted me up, I realized that what I hungered for was not just knowledge of Jesus, but Jesus Himself. My beautiful church, my kind parents, the loving camp—all were expressions and reflections of Jesus, but not Jesus Himself. My faith had convicted me of His life, but I had not let myself be rewarded with the true knowledge of my faith: Not only did Jesus live on earth two thousand years ago; He still lives through the Holy Spirit in me and in all believers. Jesus saw my earnest, though fumbling, efforts at seeking Him, and He rewarded me greatly.

A wonderful Bible teacher, ninety years young, came to teach our Bible study one day. She challenged us to teach, because by teaching we would grow in our knowledge of the Lord. I took her challenge and asked to be allowed to help lead a small group. Through the goodness of God and a mix-up of letters (that was not really coincidence), I was allowed to help with a small group, and through it Jesus changed my life. Hebrews 11:6 promises that God will reward those who earnestly seek Him, and He has richly rewarded me.

Yes, I still experience tears and sorrow, but now I have great hope and the most amazing grace! I know that Jesus lives today as He did yesterday and as He will always throughout eternity. I know that He is with me now and that one day I will be with Him in heaven, because He loved me enough to come to this earth and die for me. I am totally humbled before Him. The one for whom my heart hungered—Jesus the Christ—is my Savior, my Friend, and my Good Shepherd.

I praise You, God, for the incredible rewards You give for earnestly seeking You. It is such a joy to know you personally!

Sally Fleming

*"For I know the plans I have for you," declares
the Lord. Jeremiah 29:11*

Making Plans

Although I have been a Christian for as long as I can remember, my Bible study has drawn me closer to God in a real and intimate way. I love doing the homework for Women's Christian Bible Study and reading as part of the study. I have experienced so many "aha" moments when familiar words take on rich and deeper meaning and give me clarity I did not have before. This more intimate relationship has made me want to identify God's plan for my life and to be diligent and obedient to His call.

Not by coincidence, a friend gave me a book, *The Prayer of Jabez.* The prayer recorded in 1 Chronicles 4:9-10 really spoke to me, and I prayed Jabez's prayer every day for my children and myself. If I awakened at night, I prayed that prayer. For months I prayed that prayer day and night.

It seemed God did have plans for me. Sometime later I was asked to facilitate a small group of the Woman's Community Bible Study. My mind enumerated all the reasons I should not accept the position: my knowledge of the Bible was limited, I was not good in front of groups, and the list of excuses enlarged the territory of my terror! But somewhere deep in my soul, I felt a tug, an assuredness, and a reminder that the Bible study was not about me but about God. He was calling. How could I pray for "the God of Israel to bless me and enlarge my territory" and not answer His call? I decided to facilitate a group, counting on God to help me. As has been true of each opportunity to respond to God's plan, I have been richly blessed by this experience.

As I reflected on the past year, I suddenly realized that God didn't call me to be a facilitator because he needed me, but in His infinite wisdom and unfailing love, He called me because I needed Him.

Thank You, God, for enlarging my territory by submitting to Your plan and allowing the power of the Holy Spirit to empower me.

Marietta Gandy

*Be kind to one another, tenderhearted, forgiving one another just as
God through Christ has forgiven you. Ephesians 4:32*

A Grateful Heart

God has brought many people into my life to pray for me—
from the time of my eighth-grade confirmation, when I did not
understand what I was doing, to my college roommate, through
whom God guided me. When I was in despair over a fraternity
prank, she told me that God loved me and that His Word says to
"love your neighbor as yourself." And, as I began to obey that com-
mandment, my despair softened.

God also provided good pastors and a Christian grandmother
to teach me that "the fear of the Lord is the beginning of wisdom."
Their prayers led to my right choices. God was with me when I
made all the wrong choices for the wrong reasons. His heart broke
along with mine during the failure of my marriage. And He was
there with me even when I lived as if I did not know Him. He was
watchful when I married again—this time an older man—and was
swept into power, prestige, position, and possessions. At the same
time, He provided a friend who was being swept along also but
was grounded in her faith. This same friend invited me to her
Bible study after my severely handicapped child was born.

A few years later, this Christian friend led a discipleship group
that was ready to begin three days after the death of my father.
This wonderful support group allowed us a safe place to share our
sorrows and struggles, all the time seeking strength from God. I
was able to be with other mothers who lost children to walk with
them, to cry with them, and to bring God's love to them. Even as
my husband was diagnosed with cancer and I experienced my

own challenges with depression, God's Word had taken residence in my heart and we survived. As we went through these tragedies together, people began to notice the support we had in each other through Christ. When we opened our study to others, they began to come. God involved our group in a great movement back to Bible study. We have seen growth toward Christ in our friends and families as God's ministry spreads on tape, TV, the Internet, and books. We are constantly amazed at God's gifts to us and how He has empowered us to do his work.

In my own family, I have seen change. I have allowed God to work through my life to affect my family's faith. As my son approaches his teenage years, I see God building a backbone of faith in him. I pray this will sustain him as he begins to adopt his own identity in Christ and begins to journey toward adulthood.

I have learned through the Women's Community Bible Study not to be afraid to let God correct my plans. I am not afraid to let His forgiveness serve as my model for forgiving others. I am not afraid to give Him all praise and honor. When I look back and see all the many areas of my life that God has changed, I am left with a grateful heart.

Thank You, God, for teaching me through Your Word and Your body of believers what life in Your love resembles. I praise You for empowering me with Your Holy Spirit to reach out to a world of desperate people with that tender and gentle light. Amen.

Andrea Helfrich

I pray that you, being rooted and established in love, may have power, together with all the saints, to grasp how wide and long and high and deep is the love of Christ. Ephesians 3:17-18

Gifts from God

Where do I begin? I'm not sure I can adequately describe how my life has changed since I first joined Women's Community Bible Study. First and foremost, the Bible study introduced me to what it means to have a personal relationship with Jesus Christ, not just a religion that makes you think you are a good person. Once I understood that, blessings began to abound: forgiveness, healing, enhanced relationships, the peace that surpasses all understanding, and the gift of friendship from more Christian women than I could possibly have ever imagined.

The women of WCBS and the relationships that have developed with them have been such a sweet gift from our heavenly Father. The understandings that God has given all of us gifts and talents, that we all have extraordinary value, and that we all are part of the body of Christ uniquely positioned to fulfill His work here on earth were revolutionary to me. The unconditional love and acceptance provided within this framework of women have proved to be an invaluable gift to me.

The unique women with their unique backgrounds and life stories all contribute to God's gift to me. It was not coincidence when someone with quite similar challenges and backgrounds crossed my path. We instantly connected, and God used this individual to strengthen me in ways I cannot describe. At WCBS I found the friend that makes me laugh, the friend I walk with, the one who will drop everything and meet me to pray for an urgent need, the one who always shows interest in my family, the one who listens and never talks about herself, the one who brings soup to my door when someone is sick, the one who gently nudges me when I get off track, the one who truly makes me feel loved—my list goes on and on. I cannot think of a single need that I or my family could ever have that these incredible women could not meet. They are truly the hands, eyes, feet, and heart of Christ on this earth.

The tie that binds us all together is a love for Christ and for studying His Word together. God's level of relationships is different than the world's. He calls us to higher standards: to unconditional love and to forgiveness. He calls us to be the best that He created us to be. I have received all those benefits and more through WCBS. I only hope I can give back a measure of what I have received.

Heavenly Father, thank You for the gifts of love and friendship that come through seeking Your Son, Jesus. Amen.

Hyland Justice

The lines are fallen unto me in pleasant places;
yea, I have a goodly heritage. Psalm 16:6

A Heritage
of Faith

In 1947 an amazing thing happened in our home. My "non religious" Dad, a retired Air Force Colonel and Atlanta business owner, invited Christ into his life. A few months later, my "religious" Mother discovered through reading her Bible that she had never personally invited Christ into her life. She had believed all "about" Christ, but she had never received Him as her Savior (John 1:12).

I was two years old when my parents became Christians. I heard words like "sin" and "forgiveness" and began asking questions. My Mother and Daddy were so happy to tell me that though I was a sinner, God had provided for my sins through His Son Jesus Christ and that I could have my sins forgiven by inviting Him into my heart. At the age of four, I did invite Jesus into my life. I memorized Romans 10:9, *That if thou shalt confess with thy mouth the Lord Jesus and shalt believe in thine heart that God hath raised Him from the dead, thou shalt be saved.*

A new atmosphere pervaded our home. The focus was on sharing the "good news" of knowing Christ in a personal way and being assured of eternal life. We started having daily devotions in our home. Whenever there was a problem, Dad would say, "let's pray about it right now!" Our home became a "haven" for those who were in the ministry, and though I was an "only" child, I was never lonely. Dad's testimony and preaching as a layman and Mom's gift of Bible teaching soon became known in Christian organizations and churches throughout the U.S., and we began traveling as a family sharing the "good news." As I became proficient in playing the piano and arranging music, I would share musically the difference Christ made in my life.

My parents encouraged me to make my own decisions based on the Bible and to ask myself when faced with a decision, "What would Jesus do?" They taught me to have my own personal daily devotions and to mark a "P" by the verses that are God's promises to His children. Claiming verses became a way of life for me as difficulties came and I learned that I could always rely on my Savior and His Word.

When I met and married the man of my prayers and dreams, I learned that he, too, had a "godly heritage" as his Father upon retirement from the ministry had walked the Khyber Pass sharing Christ and ministered to persecuted Christians in Eastern bloc countries. As my husband and I have been blessed with three precious children, our fervent prayer is that they will find life's greatest joy in sharing the "good news" of Jesus Christ.

Oh Lord, let me leave my children a 'godly heritage' of faith in You and Your Word. Amen

Jackie Nims

*In the day when I cried out, you answered me; you encouraged me
with strength in my soul. (Psalm 138:3, New Living Bible)*

God's Sweet Ministry to Me

It seems like only yesterday that I asked to return to Women's Community Bible Study to co-lead a small discussion group, after I had completed a six-year comprehensive Bible study. Little did I know that my mother would become very ill only a few weeks into September, leaving me incapable of fulfilling my commitment. Naturally I felt guilty and torn, knowing that I needed to be with my mother, yet also knowing that I was placing an extra burden on the two women with whom I was to lead. What I did not realize during this critical and emotional time was that God placed me back at WCBS so He could minister to *me* through many sweet believers. Sweetest of all were my co-leaders, who prayed with and for me and graciously relieved me of all of my duties. Their genuine concern for my situation was so obvious that the guilt I felt for being unable to complete my commitment was lifted. An added blessing was that the women in our group were incredibly understanding and kind, faithfully uplifting me with prayer, flowers, cards, and phone calls.

Two months passed. Mother finally seemed to be improving after open-heart surgery when she fell and broke her shoulder. Although the doctors seemed optimistic, my dear mother continued to weaken, and finally on Christmas night, she asked me to hold her hand and slipped away to her heavenly home. I had lost my best friend, my comforter, and my encourager.

How fortunate I was to be surrounded by such loving women

during this bittersweet time, especially the beautiful woman who led our music ministry and had so deeply touched my mother through her tape ministry. Two weeks before Mother died, she had remarked that she would like this gifted person to sing at her funeral, never thinking that death was so imminent. What comfort and joy my family received during the service as this woman's beautiful voice uplifted us with songs of praise and worship, affirming God's victory over death through His Son, Jesus. This woman's ministry was a special gift to us during one of the busiest, most demanding seasons of the year. I was deeply touched when she agreed without hesitation to sing at Mother's funeral as soon as I told her of Mother's wish.

Another blessing was that my oldest son was home from college for his Christmas break. He asked to take Mother to various doctor's appointments, which allowed them some quality time together. How proud of him she was when, a few days before her death, he received his grades—a 4.0 average! She spent the final two days of her life in my home, surrounded by family who lovingly cared for her. Mother was enveloped by the strong arms of her three devoted grandsons, as well as my husband, as they helped her move about in her weakened state—what a blessing they were to her and me.

Along with my family, my dear friends in Christ have helped fill the void left by Mother's death. I will be forever grateful to God that He led me back to a precious, faith-filled group of women, even when I misunderstood His intentions. I thought He wanted me back to "work" for Him, but in His great love and mercy, He wanted me back so I could abide and rest in the love and fellowship of His believers. I will be eternally grateful!

Father, thank You for knowing, loving, and providing for me as only my Creator can. Amen.

Gayle Nix

"Be still and know that I am God." Psalm 46:10

Experiencing Grace

My life changed forever on May 3, 1998, when my beloved father suddenly died of a heart attack. Later that fall, a friend introduced me to Women's Community Bible Study, and I began an incredible journey of growth and faith. This journey was not simply the road of recovery and healing from the loss of my father; rather, it was the beginning of turning upside down my previous conceptions about what it means to believe in Jesus Christ.

I have spent much of my life as a rule follower—a law-abiding citizen, you might say. At times I resemble the elder brother of the prodigal son. At other times, I look and act like a Pharisee. I've tried, mostly through my own efforts, to be "God's girl"—doing good things through the church; working hard in my career; exposing my children and family to the proper activities; and keeping my spiritual life in order through attending church, Bible studies, and workshops. I gave my life to Christ over fifteen years ago, but I did not have the peace or rest that we are promised as believers. By 1998, I was exhausted mentally and physically from all my activity, and I was emotionally devastated by the death of my precious father.

In God's infinite wisdom, He used WCBS as one of several vehicles to make a profound impact on me. He knew that I needed to be ministered to by the Holy Spirit, and the study of Billy Graham's book on this subject changed my life. He knew that I needed a refresher course in law versus grace through our group study of Genesis and Romans. And He knew that I desperately needed conviction about Jesus, His only Son, who calls me to give up all the activity for Him and to simply abide in Him.

This call to cease much of my own and my family's endless activity has been the most radical change in my perspective to date. It is countercultural not to be busy. We all seem to define our self-worth by our schedules. But I am finding it essential in my walk with the Lord to create solitude, to be at home and available to friends and family on a regular basis, and to limit my commitments at my children's schools and at church. Jesus' gentle call to me is to stop placing my confidence and self-worth in my activities, and instead to place my confidence and my time into relationship with Him. I praise God for beginning to imprint this message on my heart through WCBS, and I trust that He who began a good work in me will be faithful to complete it.

Father, thank You for the Grace you bestow on me, allowing me to claim my identity in your Son, Jesus Christ. Amen.

Betsy Orr

I can do all things through Him who strengthens me.
Philippians 4:13 NASB

Day by Day

It is so hard for me to put into words how much it means to me to have been a member of Women's Community Bible Study for the past eight years and to express how God has made a difference in my life through this Bible study.

I grew up in a very strong Christian family; my father was a Presbyterian minister. So my background is very different from most of the other members.

I cannot remember a single time when I was not on "my walk" with Jesus as my Savior and my friend. I have never questioned my faith or God's faithfulness to me in spite of many difficult circumstances during my fifty-two years.

This wonderful community of Christian women has brought me to a deeper level of discipleship. Each year, at least one woman in my group has touched my life in a very special way. These women have exhibited strong faith and commitment to Christ in spite of their pain. They have helped me continue to keep my "light" shining for others.

During the past year I have been dealing with a deteriorating marriage and now divorce, after thirty years. Only by God's grace and the support of my Christian friends have I been able to survive.

The study this year has truly made a huge difference in my life, especially on the issue of forgiveness. My sister wrote me recently, "In the past six months, you have lived out your faith in a marvelous witness to God's promises of peace and love in the face of dire situations. Your treatment of your husband and his family in your own unimaginable pain has given new meaning to Paul's statement of love in Corinthians. You have given your children a living example of how to love others."

This shows what a difference WCBS has made in my life. A wonderful song from the musical *Godspell* helps explain how God has used this women's Bible study to draw me closer to Him:

> Day by day, O dear Lord, three things I pray:
> to see Thee more clearly,
> love Thee more dearly,
> follow Thee more nearly day by day.

Almighty God, thank You for giving us the strength we need, day by day.

Lora Smith

"For I know the thoughts and plans I have for you," says the Lord, "thoughts and plans for welfare and peace and not for evil, to give hope in your final outcome." Jeremiah 29:11

A Christmas Eve Encounter

Sometimes it takes having to sit down and specifically write about something before you realize what kind of impact it has had on your life. Years ago, on Christmas Eve, I met the leader of a Women's Community Bible Study while we were ministering in our own ways to the women at a local shelter. She invited me to sing at her Bible study, held at a large Presbyterian church. Although I originally attended only a few times a year, our relationship grew because of our love for the Father and one another. By God's grace, I was invited to lead worship on a regular basis. It was a wonderful feeling to be accepted by so many beautiful and talented women.

I grew up in a rural area outside of Athens, Georgia. Our family's conditions were meager by most standards. My father was a bookkeeper at a textile plant and worked construction job on the side. He built every house we ever lived in. My mother took care of the four children while working various jobs, including driving a school bus. Like a lot of blue-collar American families, we were God-fearing, hard-working, scrubbed behind the ears, happy children living a simple, uncomplicated life. All that changed when I started going to high school in the city. I never realized what I didn't have until my classmates started pointing it out to me. My speech was different. My clothes were different. We didn't belong to certain organizations or country clubs. In short, they excluded me, and the rejection hurt as much as anything I had ever experienced. I couldn't understand how or why people could be so mean. The wounds lasted a long time and left tender scars.

Because our Father loves us and because His Son died for our sins and to heal our wounds, I know that His Spirit guided me to that shelter on Christmas Eve. He knew I needed to feel safe and secure. He knew I needed to have loving sisters in Christ who would not reject me but would open their hearts to me so that I could be healed and rejoice in the midst of those who live in and by the love of God. The Father honored these needs by leading me to the Women's Community Bible Study.

The Bible study has changed my life, and the little ministry that God planted has started to flourish because of that Christmas Eve encounter. I have grown as a person, as a worship leader, and as a child of God through WCBS.

Most Holy Father, thank You for Your amazing love and for the blessings You have planned for me—plans for my welfare and peace, not for evil. I praise You with my whole heart and soul, and I rest in the assurance that I am blessed with Your eternal goodness and grace. In Christ's name I pray, Amen.

Paula Smith

"For I know the plans I have for you," declares the Lord, "plans to prosper you and not to harm you, plans to give you hope and a future." Jeremiah 29:11

Finding My Purpose in Life

I have always loved Jesus, ever since I was a child. I have always believed He died for me, and I have always known that He loves me. What I did not know is that He, the Creator of this universe, would pursue a relationship with me and that He alone is my purpose in this world. I did not come to this realization in a dramatic way or in one life-changing moment; rather, it was over the course of time.

I had always lived a "charmed" life with very little heartache. Aside from my parents' divorce, you could say I had led a worry-free life. In the fall of 1995, a couple of events occurred, though, that caused me to pause and question my purpose and to ask who exactly was in control of my life. It was evident that I wasn't in control!

First, my beloved father faced a major career change, not by his choice. He had loved his job since before I was born. It was the only job I had ever known for him. Seeing him hurt caused me such grief and worry.

Then a couple of months later, my grandmother suffered a stroke. She did not die; instead she was left in a conscious state, but she could not speak, eat, or do anything for herself. Memo, as we called her, personified goodness, patience, and love. Her life always reflected Jesus' love.

I found myself angry, sad, anxious, and worried over what

was happening. I remember wondering, *If God is good, then why are these bad things happening to such good people?* After pondering this for weeks and seeing these situations unfold, it dawned on me that these things happen because God is good. He knows what is best for us. Though painful at the time, the results work for our betterment, not necessarily for our comfort. Memo eventually passed away peacefully, and my father has a wonderful new career. I never saw God abandon Memo or my father. Instead, I saw Him hold their hands throughout their ordeals.

Throughout this painful time though, I truly felt like God was pursuing me, and I realized that I wanted to pursue Him too. I wanted to have a relationship with Him and wanted to know everything about Him, but where would I start?

As it happened, a friend invited me to attend Women's Community Bible Study. I was skeptical at first because I really didn't know many people, but I went. Now, seven years later, I can truly say I am a different person. My relationship with Christ has grown tremendously. God has worked wonders through the women in this group, and I feel blessed to be part of it. The Bible study has helped me know that my purpose in life is to have a relationship with my Creator, and now I know who is in control—although that still proves to be a daily struggle too!

Show us, O Lord, the way You would have us to go. May we trust in You even when that path seems unlike what we think it should be.

Julie Speyer

"Everything is possible for him who believes." Mark 9:23

Step by Step

God has been doing some major work in my life over the last eighteen months. After being single for fourteen years and living in Athens, Georgia, I decided to move to Atlanta. Both my sons were grown, so I decided it was time for a change. For some reason, Athens didn't fit my life anymore. I prayed about it, put my house up for sale and waited . . . and waited . . . and waited . . .

Ten months later, after the house had been shown many times, a couple came to the front door, and before they had looked through the entire house, they knew they wanted it. The proceedings went like clockwork. It was an exciting and frightening time, but I felt that God was leading me to make this move.

I knew that when I moved to Atlanta, I wanted to join Peachtree Presbyterian Church. I had visited frequently throughout the years and just knew that was where I needed to be. I began attending, immediately connected with a singles Sunday school class, where I easily fit in and could serve. I was happy.

Step-by-step, God led me to new areas. First I was led to become a volunteer at a rehabilitation center for spinal cord patients, when a friend's daughter was treated there for a spinal cord injury. Then God led me to Women's Community Bible Study after I heard the founder of the group speak one Sunday morning about it. I had heard about the Bible study but had not considered trying to work it into my schedule until I felt God speaking directly through her to me. I rearranged some activities and began attending. I felt at home although I didn't know any of the women in the study. I had built my life around single people, and most of these women were married or in a different age group. I didn't expect to have much in common with them except that they were Christian women. Amazingly, Christianity is all I needed to have in common with them.

As I have participated in the study and have prayed daily for my needs and the needs of others, my faith has grown incredibly. The members of my small group feel like the sisters I never had. I feel so much a part of their lives as we share and grow.

We have seen some awesome answers to prayer, and I am trying to share those miracles with all of the people with whom I come in contact. I am learning to trust that God not only has the perfect answer for others, but for me as well. I don't have to ask for the details; I just have to learn to be available, listen closely, and take a step in the direction He leads.

I hope that others will open their hearts to experience the excitement of answered prayer. I have never in my life been so sure that I am where God wants me to be. I just pray that I'll be ready for whatever the next step is.

Father, we believe that You are big enough to handle all our needs. Help us in our unbelief.

Jeannie Terry

Peace I leave with you; my peace I give you. . . .
Do not let your hearts be troubled and do not be afraid. John 14:27

A Spirit of Peace

We all love and adore our parents, but some of us are able to detach a little better than others. My father died when I was twenty-two, and my mother lived as a widow for the next thirty years. For as long as I can remember, my mother and I shared an incredibly close relationship. Her love for me was unconditional, and she extended that love to my husband and children. As a young adult, I realized how blessed I was and what a joy God allowed me in my relationship with my mother. She was so dear to me that I couldn't imagine life without her. I was terrified of losing her, and for many years I bargained with God to let me keep her a little longer.

About ten years ago, I decided I wanted to attend a Bible study. A friend invited me to attend a Christmas coffee her Bible study was hosting, and I accepted. The speaker was inspirational and the food delicious, but as lovely as it was, I thirsted for something more. The next day a dear friend called to say that there was a space in her Women's Community Bible Study small-group study for me, so I attended and have been there ever since.

As I look back on my life, I now see that God was getting me "prayed up" by sending me there. Before, I knew that I was a Christian and my faith was important to me, but I did not have the trusting relationship with Jesus that I do now. At WCBS He ministered to me and helped me mature through His Word. He reached me powerfully through the experiences, voices, tears, and love of the women there. I am so thankful for what He has seen fit to teach me, and I praise Him for whatever He has in store for me in the future.

Since I was used to being a helper and was uncomfortable in the role of someone needing help, God knew I needed work on this front. Two years ago, He took away my wonderful self-sufficiency and independence. After many complicated surgeries, many weeks in various hospitals, and a subsequent colostomy that lasted for nine months, I became dependent on everyone in my life. The women of WCBS prayed me out of the hospital, out of danger, and into the grace and total sufficiency of God's love. I still have the banners, notes, and cards I received during my five weeks in the hospital. I will never forget those smiling, beautiful, and compassionate faces. They brought me His love and strengthened my faith yet again.

Two months ago, my precious mother died. God had blessed me and granted my prayers concerning her for ninety-two years, and it seems He did not take her until He knew I was ready. He took away all fear as He revealed His presence in the room with my mother, my two daughters, and me. He took Mother's hand and led her home. The peace He left with me that night truly surpasses all human understanding.

God began preparing me for this experience ten years ago when He led me to WCBS, and I have continued to grow deeply in His Word and love. I cannot help but notice the change in my whole family as He works mightily in the hearts of those who call Him Lord.

Father, thank You that I belong to You, thank You for the peace that you give to those who believe, and for the promise that You will cover our fear with your everlasting love. You have been so faithful.

Julie Thompson

I am the true vine, and my Father is the vine grower. I am the vine, and you are the branches. Those who abide in me and I in them bear much fruit, because apart from me you can do nothing. John 15:1, 5

Growing in Faith

Spring is my favorite time of year. I love the beauty of the crab apple blossoms and redbuds in my neighborhood. I marvel at the beautiful azaleas and the majestic dogwoods. As the trees sprout new leaves and the tulips burst forth from the earth, I am reminded that spring is a time of rebirth—new life, new growth, optimism, and hope. How appropriate that Easter Sunday is in the spring! As we celebrate the victory of life over death through the resurrection of our Lord Jesus Christ, we also celebrate the power of Jesus to bring new life to all who believe in Him.

My birthday falls on the first day of spring, and I have always felt a special kinship with the season. It was also in springtime, when I was seven years old, that I invited Jesus into my heart. It was a simple act of faith, a seed planted where the Holy Spirit could take root.

The loving Christian environment that surrounded me as a child was fertile soil for my seed of faith to grow. In my family, Sunday worship was as essential as breathing, and the Scriptures and hymns I learned as a child comfort me now in times of need. But my faith was nurtured most by watching the people around me live out their Christianity day by day. I will always be especially thankful for the Christian women in my family—my mother, my older sister, my grandmothers, and my aunts—who taught me about Christ's love through their examples of goodness and kindness.

My life as a Christian has had seasons of new growth and seasons of dormancy. In high school, I hungered to know God better and began to explore the Bible for myself. As a college student, I looked to God for guidance and felt His loving hand in decisions about my friendships, my marriage, and my career. When I was in my late twenties, my husband and I lived in Italy. While I enjoyed God's handiwork in the beauty around me, I didn't spend much time with God. When I became a parent, I was back on my knees, in awe of the Creator and thankful for the precious gifts He had entrusted to our care. As a mother during these past fifteen years, I have begun to grasp the depth and passion of our heavenly Father's love for us.

Through every season, I have known that God was right there with me, just as Jesus promised (Matthew 28:20). Sometimes I have distanced myself from Him, but He has always drawn me back. At times in my life, I have felt I could not take another step without God's help. I have cried out to Him to hold me, to strengthen me, and to give me courage. He has always responded, sometimes with a visible sign of His presence, sometimes with a sense of peace in my heart, and sometimes by sending Christian friends or family members to my side.

God is the source of all my blessings, and I want to honor Him with my life. Still, my greatest challenge is to put God first every day. When I begin the day in prayer with Him and ask Him to guide my thoughts, my decisions, and my actions, amazing things happen. But it's not easy! I have a strong will and like to be in control. When I go my own way, the weeds in my life start choking out my blossoms!

What gives me hope is remembering that every day is spring for God. He gives me a fresh start every morning. Through His Son, He forgives me for the mistakes of yesterday and offers new life and new growth for today. As I seek Him through Bible study, worship, and prayer, He reveals more of Himself to me, and I grow in my love for Him. As I use my gifts for Him, He transforms me from within.

My life still has plenty of weeds. But Jesus is the vine and His Father is the vine grower. If I abide in Him and He in me, I know my seed of faith will continue to grow and bear fruit for Him.

Dear Lord, thank You for offering new life and new growth each day through Jesus, Your Son. Teach us to abide in You always.

Nancy Vason

Index

Index of Authors